Endo.

"Erin Olson has done the Church a favor in writing *Forgiveness – Unforgiveness: Revealed Through Your Fruit*s. I recommend this workbook to anyone who is willing to take an honest assessment of their lives and line it up with the truths of Scripture. With a spirit of transparency, Erin does an incredible job of using personal illustrations as well as asking challenging questions that will help you apply God's Word to your life in a very effective way."
– *Dr. Jarrett Stephens, Teaching Pastor, Prestonwood Baptist Church, Plano, TX*

"I heard it said once, 'We are never more like God than when we forgive.' In my own life, I have found that forgiveness is a decision we make and a process we walk out. Through this incredible book, Erin shares with us insights that make this journey worth every step. I highly recommend it for every believer."
- *Karen Wheaton, Director and Founder of The Ramp, Hamilton, AL*

"If you get one book this year, you will want to read this study and have it as a personal and/or ministry resource. This extraordinary offering from my friend and gifted writer, Erin Olson, unpacks the truth of how God's Word deals with both the cleansing of receiving Forgiveness and the restorative power of overcoming Unforgiveness."
- *Von Minor, Lead Pastor, Restoration Community Church, Dallas, TX*

"Erin does an excellent job of reminding us about the power of Forgiveness and the fruit of the Spirit. The self-assessments, coupled with Scripture to help start the individual transformation in our lives, is very reflective. This study reminds me that Forgiveness and redemption are around the corner for all of us."
- *Ray Maldonado, Executive, In-N-Out Burger*

FORGIVENESS – UNFORGIVENESS

Revealed Through Your Fruits

ERIN OLSON

Copyright © 2015 by Erin Olson

Forgiveness – Unforgiveness
Revealed Through Your Fruits
by Erin Olson

Printed in the United States of America
Edited by Xulon Press

ISBN 9781498424011

All rights reserved solely by the author. The author guarantees all contents are original and do not infringe upon the legal rights of any other person or work. No part of this book may be reproduced in any form without the permission of the author. The views expressed in this book are not necessarily those of the publisher.

Scripture.quotations taken from the English Standard Version (ESV). Copyright © 2001 by Crossway, a publishing ministry of Good News Publishers. Used by permission. All rights reserved.

www.xulonpress.com

Contents

Dedication vii
About the Author ix

Week One – Introduction: Offense Doesn't Win Games 11
Week Two – Love/Hate 18
Week Three – Joy/Sadness 30
Week Four – Peace/Disorder 40
Week Five – Patience/Impatience 53
Week Six – Kindness/Unkindness 60
Week Seven – Goodness/Evil 69
Week Eight – Faithfulness/Disloyalty 76
Week Nine – Gentleness/Abruptness 86
Week Ten – Self-control/Rashness 98

Leader Guide and Discussion Questions 109
Endnotes 115

Dedication

I dedicate this study to my Lord and Savior. Without Him, I would never have been able to understand what true forgiveness is. He gave me life, and I am forever humbled and blessed.

Thank you to my husband, Scott, for supporting the talents and gifts that God has given me and extending forgiveness when I am preoccupied and still have not learned to compile a "to-do" list.

About the Author

Honestly, never in her wildest dreams did Erin Olson ever think she would be writing about Jesus. "Really, are you kidding me?" she laughs. But when Jesus gets a hold of your heart, it is hard to let Him go. Without Him, your heart is missing something. You may or may not know what that something is, but when you have Him, you just know.

Erin grew up going to church but was far from what she considers a "church girl." She didn't give much thought to God six days and twenty-three hours per week. She was a "one-hour-a-week churchgoer." Nothing more, nothing less. She was fortunate in that she knew who God was, accepted it, and understood it (at least she thought she did). She never doubted for a minute who the Creator was, she just denied Him ... *all the time.* She really had no idea that He was the person she had been searching and longing for.

"I had no concept of the enormity of the Cross. I knew of God, but I didn't know Jesus," she says.

She made bad choices. They scaled in degrees of how bad they were, but, nevertheless, they were bad. Eventually, she ran from her hometown and from all that she knew to a new state and a new life. She did not know anyone, did not have a job lined up, and did not know the best part of town to live in. However, it ended up to be a place where God eventually led her to her husband and subsequent building of her family. It was also during this process of searching that she found Jesus—and her life was changed forever.

Her goal in all of this is to glorify God, not herself. If she could completely remove herself from this, she would, but she cannot. You see, we all have a story, one that is unique to us. "Don't get me wrong; Jesus does not need an opening act by any means," she says, "But what He likes to do best is to use ordinary people to do extraordinary things. He uses the least of us, and oftentimes some of the most messed up, to magnify Him."

Erin Olson's full-time job as a homemaker consists of serving her husband, Scott, her three children, and three dogs. Erin writes a Christian blog for her ministry, Sandalfeet Ministries (www.sandalfeet.org), and loves to teach the Word of God. Erin serves in the women's and children's ministries, as well as helps her husband with a Bible Fellowship class at their church home, Prestonwood Baptist Church. She serves as a prayer ministry leader for her children's school, Prestonwood Christian Academy, among many other volunteer duties there. Many ministries and missionaries around the world have her heart, as well.

Prior to staying at home, Erin worked as a corporate/intellectual property paralegal for large law firms and corporations for almost a decade.

Erin holds a bachelor's degree in Business Administration from Regis University (Denver, CO) and a master's degree in Christian Leadership from Liberty Baptist Theological Seminary (Lynchburg, VA).

Week One

Introduction

Offense Doesn't Win Games

Experts might say that the best drivers are those who drive defensively. You know the kind I am talking about. These drivers are always scanning the road ahead, next to them, behind them—always wondering what the other person might do. My husband is one of these defensive-driver types. There are even "Defensive Driving" courses. However, it is the opposite of how we think, or at least how I think (I also have a problem with credit/debits so it could just be my brain that works this way). Most would say that this is driving offensively, right? I mean you are the one in control of the car, like a quarterback with the football, and you get to decide where your car is going.

The same goes with life. Most people you ask would say they live a defensive life. They erect walls around their hearts and their lives. Their tough exterior speaks volumes about the hurt they have endured in their lifetime. As with driving, while we think we are living defensively, we are actually living offensively. We have not been able to let go of offenses that weigh us down, and offense does not win ball games.

Given time, those offensive weights will drag you down into pits of despair.

It is not a matter of *if* someone will offend you; rather, it is a matter of *when* and how many times. How will you let the offense affect you? Being offended is part of living in a broken world, full of broken and selfish people. The shocking part for some of us is that we are walking around bound to shackles of unforgiveness, and we do not even realize it. We stuff and we push, but we do not release.

The first book I read after finally surrendering my life to Jesus Christ was a book by John Bevere titled, *The Bait of Satan; Living Free from the Deadly Trap of Offense.* I remember reading this and thinking that I had been slapped across the face with a truth that I had been running from my whole life. By allowing the sin of unforgiveness to dwell in my soul, I was allowing gaping holes to be propped open for Satan himself to reside in. Quite frankly, I was shocked. I had made some not-so-good choices as a young adult and dabbled in sinful activities, but I would not have classified myself as a person in whom Satan was residing; that is, until I read this book. As I read through the pages, my eyes were opened to a whole other realm—the spiritual realm—the place where believers and Satan's army are doing battle.

> Put on the whole armor of God, that you may be able to stand against the schemes of the devil. For we do not wrestle against flesh and blood, but against the rulers, against the authorities, against the cosmic powers over this present darkness, against the spiritual forces of evil in the heavenly places (Eph. 6:11–12).

Introduction

Satan likes nothing better than to get you to a place of living outside of the will of God for your life. He does not want you to operate in the Spirit. Instead, Satan wants to feed you lies.

One of the simple tests to determine whether or not you are walking around in a state of unforgiveness is to review the list of the nine attributes of the fruit of the Spirit found in Galatians 5:22–23: "But the Holy Spirit produces this kind of fruit in our lives: love, joy, peace, patience, kindness, goodness, faithfulness, gentleness and self-control." Does your life reflect these things? If you have been walking around in unforgiveness, I would argue that the answer is probably "No!"

Over the course of the next nine weeks, we are going to look at each attribute of the fruit individually and see what the counterfeit looks like for each. There will be a lot of self-discovery involved, as well as some deep-seated emotions coming to the surface. I want you to know that it is okay!

In order to start, you will need to answer a few questions first. We must first know where we are, where we are going, and the obstacles that might be in the way. Think of it like a navigation system in your car or on your iPhone. If you do not know the coordinates, you have no idea where you are or where you will end up.

Some of you may or may not know the answer to the following question, but it is an important question.

If you were to die right now, would you know for sure that you were going to Heaven? Yes or No? Why did you give that response? What are you basing that on?

_____

_____

_____

It is important to know the answer to this question because unless you have trusted in Jesus as your Lord and Savior, you cannot possess the Holy Spirit. How do I know this? Let's take a look at John 14:15–17:

> If you love me, obey my commandments. And I will ask the Father and He will give you another Advocate who will never leave you. He is the Holy Spirit who leads into all truth. The world cannot receive Him because it isn't looking for Him and doesn't recognize Him. But you know Him, because He lives with you now and later He will be in you.

If your answer to the above question was "Yes, because I believe that Jesus Christ was born, crucified and resurrected and coming again," I am excited to lock arms with you. If your answer to the above was "Maybe," "No," or "I am not sure," then I am also excited for you. That means that God has you in the right place, and He is probably about to rock your world!

There is only one way to Heaven. It is not about anything we do or strive for. Ephesians 2:8–9 says, "For by grace you have been saved through faith. And this is not your own doing; it is the gift of God, not a result of works, so that no one may boast."

Why do I think it is important to start a Bible study about forgiveness with determining where your salvation lies? Two reasons: one is that Jesus died for the forgiveness of sins. Outside of a relationship with Jesus, we cannot even begin to fathom the concept of forgiveness and we ourselves are not fully forgiven. The second is that, outside of a relationship with Jesus Christ, we are operating under our own authority instead of operating in the power of the Holy Spirit.

Jesus says in John 14:6, "I am the Way, the Truth and the Life. No one comes to the Father except through Me." You can believe in God all day

Introduction

long, but unless you believe that Jesus is your Lord and Savior, then you are walking through the wide gate instead of entering through the narrow gate.[1]

Let's take a look at the fruit of the Spirit again. Next to each attribute, write a description about how you feel about this particular fruit in your life (i.e., overflowing, needs improvement, nonexistent, struggling, etc.).

Love: _____

Joy: _____

Peace: _____

Patience: _____

Kindness: _____

Goodness: _____

Faithfulness: _____

Gentleness: _____

Self-control: _____

Dear readers, I do not know what your list looks like, but let me tell you, my list has not always been fruitful. There have been plenty of years where there were droughts, insect infestations, and bad soil. Instead of producing good things—fruitful things—I was carrying around and displaying the counterfeit of these fruitful things. For each good fruit of the Spirit, there is a bad fruit, if you will, represented by the evil one himself. Look at the words above again. Don't they just sound like what Heaven is like? I can hear the hummingbirds, see perfectly blue skies, and see smiling faces.

Now, let's take a look at the counterfeit fruits planted by the evil one himself. Look at this list and make some notes next to each word. Are you experiencing any of these things in your life?

Hate: _____

Sadness: _____

Disorder: _____

Impatience: _____

Unkindness: _____

Immorality: _____

Disloyalty: _____

Abruptness: _____

Rashness: _____

These words just sound ugly. They sound like the things that go bump in the night.

We are going to spend some time over the next nine weeks and find a way to harvest good fruit together. It is going to be a process of pruning away anything that is not good so that the good can sprout forth.

Introduction

Start here by asking God to speak to you and show you who in your life you to need to seek forgiveness from or perhaps who you need to extend forgiveness to.

Pray a simple prayer like this:

> *Father, You are the one who has the ability to forgive me. Jesus, as He hung on that cross for my sins, asked You to forgive each one of us. He taught us to pray in the Lord's Prayer, "Forgive us our trespasses as we forgive those who trespass against us." Lord, show me who it is that I need to forgive and who I need to offer forgiveness to. I want to bear the fruit that You have already promised to me. Convict me, Holy Spirit, of where I am not offering forgiveness. Push back the darkness from my life and shine Light where it is needed. In Jesus' name, Amen.*

As the Holy Spirit convicts you this week, use the space below to write out the names of those whom He brings to mind and why it is that you need to forgive or offer forgiveness. You will probably need to visit this list often as we continue through this study.

Name   Why

_____

_____

_____

_____

Week Two

Love / Hate

I have a "love–hate relationship" with so-and-so. Have you ever said or heard anyone say anything like this? How can you love something and hate something? They are total opposites.

What does love mean? *Love* is defined as a "strong affection for another arising out of kinship or personal ties; affection based on admiration; warm enthusiasm or devotion; and an unselfish loyal and benevolent concern for the good of another,"[2] among other things.

Hate, on the other hand is defined as "intense hostility and aversion, deriving from fear, anger or sense of injury; and extreme dislike or antipathy."[3]

Below, list the people or things that you love.

_____

_____

Love / Hate

Why do you love these people or things?

_____

_____

With regard to the people you say you love, do they feel the same way about you?

_____

_____

How do you feel when they do not?

_____

_____

Now, list the people or things you hate/dislike.

_____

_____

Why do you feel this way?

_____

_____

Can you pinpoint a specific event that caused you to feel this way?

_____

Nobody wants to walk around feeling unloved. Do you remember when you were in junior high school and all of your friends suddenly, without warning, stopped talking to you? You felt like no one liked you, and everyone hated you.

The Beatles sang in their song,

> All you need is love
> All you need is love
> All you need is love, love
> Love is all you need

You know who else said this long before The Beatles did? Jesus. The Pharisees were trying to trap Jesus with a question so they asked Him this, "Which is the most important commandment in the law of Moses?"[4]

Jesus replied, "Love the Lord your God with all of your heart, soul and mind."[5] Of course the Pharisees agreed with this because it lined up with the First Commandment given to Moses in Exodus 20:3, "You shall have no other gods before me." But the second, and according to Jesus equally important commandment, is "Love your neighbor as yourself."[6] This has affectionately been named the "Golden Rule" or "do unto others as you'd have done unto you." The Berenstain Bears have a book with that title that my youngest son just adores.

So if we walk around loving others, we would expect others to be loving toward us. However, if we walk around hating others, we would expect others to hate us, right? Yes ... well, sort of. We cannot be responsible for other people's actions toward us. We can only be responsible for our actions toward others.

I do not know about your household, but my children are not allowed to use the word *hate*. I catch myself saying the "H" word sometimes, and then I have to mentally reprimand myself. I tell my children that "hate" is a very strong word and that I would rather them say instead, "I do not like." Hate is harsh. The Bible tells us in Proverbs 10:12, "Hatred stirs up quarrels, but love makes up for all offenses."

It is hard to love someone who has hurt you. It is hard to love someone who has betrayed you. It is hard to love someone who does not love you back the way you want. It is hard to love someone who has harmed you. But it is what Jesus requires of us. Why? Because the love of God is unconditional upon anything we do or do not do. God desires for us to walk in the freedom that extending love provides.

Jesus told us in John 13:34–35, "So now I am giving you a new commandment: Love each other. *Just as I have loved you,* you should love each other. Your love for one another will prove to the world that you are my disciples" (emphasis mine).

In the original Greek, the word αγαπη (agape) is used throughout for the word *love*. Agape-type love, according to 1 Corinthians 13, is love that is kind, does not display unseemly behavior, hates evil, is associated with honesty, and protects, as well as a few other attributes. This is the type of love Jesus has for you. As Christ followers, our goal is to become more Christ-like. If Jesus loves you with this type of love, we should love others in the same manner. But do we?

Describe a time when you felt like you were not loved.

_____

_____

Do you think that Jesus still loved you during this instance? Why or why not?

_____

_____

_____

Now, describe a time when you felt like you could not love a certain person for something they did or said. What happened to cause you to feel this way?

_____

_____

_____

Do you think God loved that person any differently during this same time period? Why or why not?

_____

_____

_____

We can walk through any given day and be hurt by people. Someone can look at us wrong or say something that perhaps rubs us the wrong way, and sometimes people do atrocious things to us or to the people we love. Those hurts, if not dealt with properly, can turn to anger, hate, and bitterness.

Those small pebbles of emotions can build up and turn into large boulders in our souls that can render the Holy Spirit ineffective in our lives. The Apostle John wrote in 1 John 4:20, "If someone says, 'I love God,' but hates a [Christian] brother or sister, that person is a liar; for if we don't love people we can see, how can we love God, whom we cannot see?" Ouch. The Apostle John is telling us then that if we hate someone, then we cannot love God because we do not love people the way He loves people. This stings because I want to love the Lord God with all my heart, even if that means loving people that the world says that I do not have to love.

The best example of this kind of godly love can often be found in the courtroom. During those difficult times when family members and victims have to present a statement to a defendant in a courtroom are some of those moments when you can see God best at work. We can tell a lot about a person when they present their statement to the defendant. Those who are filled with hate, spitfire, and anger toward the defendant have not fully gotten to a point where they can extend love and forgiveness. They are trapped in unforgiveness in that moment, and the devil knows it. On the other hand, those family members and victims who can say they have chosen to forgive that person in love have put aside their emotions, wills and desires and have given it all to the Lord to handle—and the Lord always handles it in love. God said to the grumbling, sinful Israelites in Malachi 1:2, "I have always loved you."

Hatred, which is not a fruit of the Spirit, according to Proverbs 10:12, stirs up strife and quarrels. The only way to undo a strife or quarrel is to extend forgiveness. That is hard to do when you are not the one who caused the offense, but it must be done.

I do not know who originally said this, but it is a great quote.

> *Forgiveness doesn't make the other person right; forgiveness sets you free.*

Part of that forgiveness is getting to a point where you do not hate or dislike someone, but instead love him or her as your Lord loves them. We cannot hold hate in our heart. It must be released as we extend forgiveness. The Lord told Moses in Leviticus 19:17–18, "Do not nurse hatred in your heart for any of your relatives. Confront people directly so you will not be held guilty for their sin. Do not seek revenge or bear a grudge against a fellow Israelite, but love your neighbor as yourself." Hate leads to a grudge that can bear *violent* fruit and that fruit is definitely not of the Holy Spirit. Love, on the other hand, is the cornerstone for biblical ethics in both the Old Testament and the New Testament.

Have you ever held a grudge against anyone?

_____

_____

Describe what your life looked like during that season.

_____

Are you still holding a grudge against someone?

_____

_____

Why?

_____

If you were to forgive that person, what do you think that would do for you? For your current life situation? Are you willing to forgive that person?

_____

_____

_____

_____

If so, ask the Lord how you should go about extending forgiveness. Does He want you to write it down here, or does He want you to send a letter? Does He want you to call that person, or does He want you to meet that person face-to-face?

I had to do this recently – not on the witness stand, but through a form of modern technology – Facebook. I wrote in a blog back in April 2012 (see sidebar) about some spiritual cleaning God had been asking me to do with regard to forgiveness. There was a person God had been asking me to extend forgiveness to. I had been holding onto that unforgiveness for over twenty-two years. I did not outwardly hate this person (probably because I had not had contact with this person for more than twenty years), but I was holding hate inside my heart for this person and what had transpired. God was not going to stand any longer for me to hate this person or myself about what had happened, so He asked me to let this person know. You can read how that worked out in my blog post, but let me assure you, the moment I hit "Send," a weight had been lifted off of my spirit and it has never returned.

From the Sandalfeet blog
"Building Out the Attic"—April 26, 2012, By Erin Olson

I have been doing some spiritual cleaning over the last couple of years. It hasn't been a spring-like cleaning as a new season approaches. Rather, I have been doing the deep kind of attic cleaning that comes right before a major move. This cleaning has taken me into places I never thought I would revisit, but I have. I've been cleaning out the bins of anger, shame, guilt, pride, idolatry, and the biggest bin of all, at least for me, forgiveness. Now, this isn't to say that I have conquered all of these bins, but I have opened them up, taken inventory of their contents, and made provision, or requested assistance, for what to do with those contents. It is not an easy task and not for the faint of heart.

This week, I believe I have finally unpacked the final bin of forgiveness. As I said, this one was hard for me. I have really had to pray over whom I needed to forgive and whether or not I needed to go to that person and let them know of my forgiveness. The acts that needed to be forgiven ranged from petty to monumental. Some I have just handed over to the Lord, but others, the Lord has required me to go to. Talk about humbling—and, for a stubborn soul like me, downright irritating at times.

I have wrestled with God about some of the people He has laid on my heart. I have said stuff to Him like, "Seriously, I have to go to her? But, she was the one who did that to me!" or "But, what if they don't think they did anything wrong? What is their response going to be? Aren't I just setting myself up to be hurt again?" I really am thankful that God is so patient with me! In His loving tone, He kept whispering to me the words from 2 Corinthians 5:18–20:

> And all of this is a gift from God, who brought us back to Himself through Christ. And God has given us this task of

reconciling people to Him. For God was in Christ, reconciling the world to Himself, no longer counting people's sins against them. And He gave us this wonderful message of reconciliation. So we are Christ's ambassadors; God is making His appeal through us. We speak for Christ when we plead, 'Come back to God!'

I have sometimes seen forgiveness as a self-serving thing. I feel better if I extend forgiveness, and then the ball is in that person's court, or I think it will make that person feel better so it is a win-win situation for us all. But, because of God and this passage, I realize that my forgiveness (whether I am giving or receiving) is not about me at all. It is actually about God and for God. If I can't be relieved of the burden of forgiveness, I can't be fully reconciled with God, so there is going to be some road blockage between the Father and me. Because all of my spiritual cleaning is really for my Father, I certainly do not want to create any obstacles.

As part of this cleaning, I have extended forgiveness that has not always been met with the expectation or hope that I wanted. Some have ignored the particular problem all together and turned it back to me (boy, let me tell you how hard that was to swallow) and some, like this week, have been glorious.

The forgiveness that I extended this week was a long-time coming. It had lingered for years and was an act against me that some would say is unforgivable. It was the kind of act that rocked my world and changed my life. It was an act that was wrapped around guilt and shame on my part because had I done some things differently, it probably could have been avoided. For a moment in my life, it defined me. I hated that, I hated the person and I hated myself. So this was a big one, and this one name was the last one on my forgiveness list. God was telling me that He needed me to take care of it ... now. Colossians 3:13 says, "Make allowance for each other's faults, and forgive anyone who offends you. Remember, the Lord forgave you, so you must forgive others." Forgiveness clearly is not an option; it is a command, and God was ordering me to do it.

Up until recently, I had no way of contacting this person (I had a great excuse then, right?), but thanks to modern technology, I now had a way to reach out. Great. After much prayer this past Tuesday morning, I prepared my message. It was very simple and to the point. In my message, I extended forgiveness, shared with this person that I know Jesus has forgiven me, and shared that Jesus can forgive them, too (I did not know whether this person had a relationship with Christ, but I wanted to stay in keeping with 2 Corinthians 5:18-20). I stared at the message for several minutes before I finally just closed my eyes, said a prayer (something to the effect of, "Lord, I will accept whatever response comes.") and pressed "Send." It was in the Lord's hands at that point.

The response I got mere minutes later was nothing what I thought it was going to be, but everything I had hoped it would be. Not only had I released that ugly ball of hate, anger, and sadness, but also the person on the receiving end of the forgiveness was able to release their own ball of whatever it was that they had been holding. From the tone of the message, I could sense that this had eaten away at this person just as much as it had eaten at me all of these years.

God, once again, was victorious!

I am happy to report that my attic is almost empty and instead of filling it back up, I want to build it out so it can never be cluttered again. I want it to be filled with life and not junk. My load has truly been lightened!

For some of you, you may have more than one person to forgive. I would encourage you to pray about each person/instance specifically because God does not always have you handle every situation the same.

God does not want us to walk in hate or dislike; He wants us to walk in love. If we are walking in the fruit of the Spirit, we need to be walking in the

Light. Look up 1 John 2:11. In your own words, write down what this verse means in your life. Feel free to put specific names in place of "brother and sister" and insert your name in place of "such a person."

_____

_____

_____

_____

A few years back while I was exiting the carpool lane, I noticed one of my sweet momma friends in front of me had a taillight out. I dialed her cell phone (hands-free of course!) and told her that her taillight was out. She said, "Thank you. I would have had no idea."

Friends, for some of you, I am giving that call to you right now. Unforgiveness is causing you to live with your Light out. Sure, for some of you it might be a low dim, a flickering. But for others, your Light may be completely out. Forgiveness fixes that.

> *Father in Heaven, the Lord's Prayer tells us, "Forgive us our trespasses as we forgive those who trespass against us." You would not have taught us to pray this prayer unless you wanted us to seek your forgiveness, as well as to forgive others. Lord, may the Holy Spirit be awakened in my soul and may the Spirit help me to see whom I do not love well. May the Spirit shine Light on my unforgiveness and any hate or dislike I am holding on to. Lord, may I be a willing vessel to be used by You always. In Jesus' name, Amen.*

Week Three

Joy / Sadness

According to depression statistics from the Centers for Disease Control and Prevention (CDC), about nine percent of adult Americans have feelings of hopelessness, despondency, and/or guilt that generate a diagnosis of depression. At any given time, about three percent of adults have major depression, also known as major depressive disorder, a long-lasting and severe form of depression. In fact, major depression is the leading cause of disability for Americans between the ages of 15 and 44, according to the CDC. Understanding these very real depression statistics helps paint a fuller picture of the impact of depression in America.[7]

Quite frankly, it is sad that so many people are so sad. Sadness comes from many things. The definition of *sad* is "affected with or expressive of grief or unhappiness,"[8] whereas the definition of *joy* is "a feeling of great happiness."[9] In our modern culture, happiness has taken on a different definition. Modern culture has defined happiness as whatever pleases us, whatever feeds our emotional needs or fulfills our desires.

Name some of the things that cause you joy.

_____

_____

_____

Name some of the things that cause you sadness.

_____

_____

_____

Why do these things cause you sadness?

_____

_____

_____

Corrie ten Boom in her book, *The Hiding Place,* said, "Joy runs deeper than despair." She should know. Corrie and her family were arrested for being Jewish sympathizers. Her family was taken from their home and sent to a concentration camp. Those who did not pass away on the way to the concentration camp eventually died in the concentration camp, including her beloved sister Betsie. Corrie ten Boom knew what it was to live in despair; she endured deplorable conditions because she chose to be kind and love others. She lost family members because they chose Jesus over the ways of the world. She also chose to forgive those who had taken so much from her. She had joy because she had Jesus. She would go on to say, "Happiness isn't something that depends on our surroundings ... It's something we make inside ourselves."

To have joy in any given situation is a choice. It is also what the Holy Spirit desires for you.

I love this definition of joy:

Jesus.

Others.

You (Self).

When we have Jesus at the forefront of everything we do, it should not be hard to love others, forgive others, and serve others before ourselves.

Is it hard to be joyful in tough situations? To some yes, but to others no.

My dear, sweet spiritual momma lost an adult son to a sudden heart attack three years ago. It was a shock to say the least. Was she sad? Of course. Is she still sad? Yes. But what most people cannot understand is how she can still have so much joy. How can she love and serve a God who would take her son in his prime with a wife and two young children? It is because she has the joy that comes from having complete trust and faith in her Lord. Job said it best when he said, "the Lord gave me what I had and the Lord has taken it away." [10]

Joy / Sadness

> So with you: Now is your time of grief, but I will see you again and you will rejoice, and no one will take away your joy (John 16:22).

How many times has it been someone that you care deeply about who has hurt you the most? How much harder is it to forgive someone that you love and care deeply about than to forgive a stranger? Yes, there are some who are angry with God Himself and cannot bring themselves to forgive Him.

Holding on to unforgiveness causes us to live in sadness, in despair, and do things we normally would not do. We are sad for what could have been, for what should have been, or for what we deemed right. The sadness will cause us to withdraw from that person and from situations and get us to a place of isolation. Sadness feeds itself in dark, lonely places whereas joy lives best in the light.

Look up John 15:10–12. In your own words, write what Jesus was telling his disciples.

_____

_____

_____

Different translations say that your joy will be "complete" or "overflow." Part of the meaning of the word *blessed* means "to be happy, joyful, and depression free." Read Matthew 5:3–11.

After reading these verses, would you define yourself as being truly blessed? Why or why not?

Do you think your circumstances or your attitude are causing you to not feel *blessed*? Why or why not?

When David was in hiding from Saul, he had every reason to feel despair, sadness, anger, and bitterness. While David did on occasion voice his displeasure to God, he also gave God much praise and worship and proclaimed that he would live in joy. "Then my head will be exalted above the enemies who surround me; at his tabernacle I will sacrifice with shouts of joy; I will sing and make music to the Lord" (Ps. 27:6).

Ronald F. Youngblood in *Nelson's New Illustrated Bible Dictionary* said,

> Even when David's enemies were hunting him down and closing in, he was able to compose joyful psalms of praise to God. He rejoiced in his understanding that God, His Father, could flatten any army, resolve any conflict, and confuse the plans of those who sought to kill him. He was joyful in the Lord (emphasis mine).

Did you see that statement in there? The one that says that God could "resolve any conflict." Conflict resolution is intentional. It is a process. During seminary, I had to write a paper on conflict resolution. I had to choose someone I was having difficulty with and create a plan to resolve the conflict that was stirring up not-so-great feelings. Why does it matter if we resolve conflict? Because if we do not, the root of bitterness will grow. Feelings will inevitably get hurt, and a state of unforgiveness will lead into negative feelings toward that person.

How do you handle conflict resolution? Do you handle it immediately, stew over it a while, pray about it, or brush it under the rug and hope it goes away?

_____

_____

_____

In Matthew 5:23–24, what does Jesus tell us to do first?

_____

_____

Is that usually your first response?

_____

_____

If your answer is no, your current life situation could be proof of how you handle forgiveness.

Fred Luskin, PhD, health psychologist at Stanford University, says this, "Not forgiving—nursing a grudge—is so caustic, it raises your blood pressure, depletes your immune function, makes you more depressed and causes enormous physical stress to the whole body." I would also add that unforgiveness completely robs you of joy.

For a moment, I want to talk only to those of you who loathe family gatherings because of some longtime family issue. Additionally, I would like to talk to those of you who are having trouble at work with a demanding, unkind employer or fellow worker. Finally, I would like to talk to those of you who have difficult or insensitive friends or family members or acquaintances that are anything but sensible. Okay, great ... I have everyone's attention now!

See, we all walk around every day with people who have hurt us or who have the potential to somehow hurt us (whether that may be physical hurts or emotional hurts). Aside from moving far, far away from civilization, we cannot avoid this. James in James 1:2 said, "Consider it all joy, my brothers, whenever you face trials of many kinds." Those trials include difficult life situations and people. We are to find joy and be joyful in *all* circumstances. In the Greek language, the word *consider* is *hēgeomai*, which means, "to lead." So James was telling the people *to lead with joy* in all things and at all times, and yes, the trials are *when* not *if*.

Many of us walk around sad, depressed, and negative because we are holding on to something. We need to let that go. We need to resolve today to forgive those who have hurt us. We also need to pray for those who continue to hurt us (although I would advise that if you are in a situation that is not healthy or safe, please seek help immediately).

First Corinthians 15:33 says, "Don't be fooled by those who say such things, for 'bad company corrupts good character.'" Paul is talking about many "things" in this passage, but the "bad company" he is referring to are people who are evil, negative, and poisonous. We do not ever want to be the one whom people consider "bad company." We do not want to be the one who is negative and bitter all the time. We want to be joy-filled believers and great witnesses for the Lord.

When you think of a negative, bitter person, who is the first person that comes to your mind?

_____

Why do you think this person is perceived this way? Do you know why this person is this way?

_____

_____

When people think of you, what are some of the adjectives they would use to describe you?

_____

_____

Ask a couple of friends or close family members how they would describe you and jot down those comments here. Were you surprised by any of their comments?

_____

The prophet Micah goes on a little bit of a rant in Micah 7 about his enemies and the people around him. It was written long before the gospel of grace (thank you, Jesus!), but toward the end of his long-winded, round-about sort-of-way of forgiveness to his enemies, he said this,

> Where is another God like you, who pardons the sins of the survivors among his people? You cannot stay angry with your people forever, because you delight in showing mercy. Once again you will have compassion on us. You will trample our sins under your feet and throw them into the depths of the ocean (Micah 7:18–19)!

If God can forgive us and throw all of our stuff into the deepest depths of the ocean, why are we not able to do that as well? Is He calling you to throw some stuff into the depths of the ocean today?

List it here.

_____

_____

_____

God wants you to live a life of overflowing joy, not sadness, despair, or depression. He wants you to forgive those who need forgiveness and love those who are difficult to love. He wants you to live in the power of forgiveness that He has extended to you through Jesus. Romans 15:13 says that God fills you with joy and peace and He wants you to overflow with hope by the power of the Holy Spirit. That is my prayer for you too.

Father, You know the hurts I have suffered. You know the heaviness of my sadness and my despair. Your Word tells me to come to You with my heavy burdens, and You will give me rest. Father, today I release my burdens of unforgiveness to You. I do not want to carry them anymore. My spirit cannot walk in sadness and joy at the same time, and I only want to walk in joy for You all the days of my life. Proverbs 17:22 says, "A cheerful heart is good medicine, but a broken heart saps a person's strength." Lord, heal my heart today and restore it to complete fullness of joy. Give me the strength that only You can give me. In Jesus' name, Amen.

Week Four

Peace / Disorder

"Forgive me for picking back up what I've already laid at your feet" (Author Unknown). Is this something you struggle with? Yes, me too—at least I used to in a very big way, and I think I know why. At one time, I lived wrapped up in religion instead of grace. I lived a life that said I identified as a "Christian," yet I didn't have a personal relationship with Jesus. Do you know how I know this? I had no peace.

Let's remind ourselves that we are walking through the fruit of the Spirit as defined in Galatians 5:22–23: "But the Holy Spirit produces this kind of fruit in our lives: love, joy, *peace*, patience, kindness, goodness, faithfulness, gentleness and self-control" (emphasis mine).

I had no peace because it is the Holy Spirit that gives peace, and I did not have the Holy Spirit because I did not *know* and *accept* Jesus as my Lord and Savior. I had not allowed myself to receive the gift of grace that God was trying to give me (Eph. 2:8–9). Because Jesus was not Lord and Savior of my life, I was not operating in the power of the Holy Spirit (Eph. 1:13). I was bearing my own fruit instead of His fruit—and my own fertilizer stunk (pun intended!).

Ironically, my name in Gaelic (Irish) means "peace." Yet up until the moment I surrendered to Jesus, I had more disorder and chaos than peace in my life (see the following sidebar). Sure, it may not have looked like that on the outside, but my insides were torn up.

From the Sandalfeet blog
"What's in a Name?"—February 21, 2013, by Erin Olson

Historically, names meant a lot. Today, the "naming" industry makes tons of money selling books about naming your baby. Every year, the top 100 boy and girl names are released. Tabloids trip over themselves to figure out the names of celebrity babies. Some people choose family names. Some choose popular names. Some choose creative names. No matter what, we all have a name.

This past week I was working on a Bible study by Tony Evans titled, *It's Not Too Late – How God Uses Less Than Perfect People*. The lesson for the week was Jacob. Some of you know Jacob's story, but for those who do not, here's an abbreviated version of Genesis 25–29.

Jacob was born to Rebekah and Isaac. He had a twin brother, Esau, with whom he struggled even while in the womb, and during the birthing process, Jacob grabbed Esau's heel as if to stop him from being born first. Out of the womb, Jacob had some control issues. While Rebekah was pregnant, God had told her that her youngest son would be exalted over the older son, which was totally opposite to what was customary in that day. The older son always got the biggest and best blessing. Jacob devised a plan one day to steal his brother's blessing. Esau did not make the process very difficult for him because he was not a traditionalist—at least he did not think he was until it was too late. As Isaac, their daddy, lay on his deathbed, Rebekah and Jacob devised one last plan to dupe Isaac into believing that Jacob was Esau so Isaac could pass the blessing to Jacob before he died. The plan worked, and Jacob received the blessing. Esau found out and let's just say, he was not a happy camper and threatened to kill Jacob.

Jacob had to flee for his life into the wilderness to go to a faraway land to live with his Uncle Laban. While Jacob was there, he met a girl and wanted to marry her. He worked seven years for free in order to marry Rachel, his beloved. When it was time to receive Rachel as his wife, Laban pulled a trick over on Jacob and instead gave him Rachel's sister, Leah, who was definitely not who Jacob wanted. So the trickster had been tricked himself.

Fast forward fourteen years and Jacob wanted to take his family, leave Laban, and return home. Jacob realized that God had blessed him while with Laban. He had wives, children, and his fields were profitable. This was not only benefiting him, but Laban knew he was making profits from it, too. Laban's family was accusing Jacob of stealing their wealth. The Lord told Jacob to return to his homeland, so Jacob and his family fled.

The story could have stopped here. Jacob fled and returned home and every one lived happily ever after. Remember, Esau, Jacob's brother wanted to kill him for what he did. Esau got word that Jacob was returning home, and so Esau assembled a group of four hundred men. This homecoming was not to Jacob's liking, so he sent his family one way and his servants ahead to provide gifts to Esau. With everyone gone, Jacob spent the night in the wilderness by himself. Jacob prayed and said, "God, I know you promised to take care of me. Please protect me from my brother Esau" (see Genesis 32:9–12).

That night, Jacob wrestled with a man all night long. Right before the breaking of the dawn, the man said to Jacob, "What is your name?" Jacob replied, "Jacob." "Your name will no longer be Jacob," the man told him. "From now on you will be called Israel, because you have fought with God and with men and have won." Jacob said, "Please tell me your name." The man said, "Why do you want to know my name?" And then he blessed Jacob (Genesis 32:26–30). Why in the world did Jacob care what the guy's name was? Did it matter? What purpose did it serve?

Getting back to the point of names. Jacob's name meant "trickster." He lived up to his name for sure during his younger years. But after being cheated, lied to, chased, wanted for dead, and left totally alone wrestling with God, he had grown wiser. The name Israel means "God fights." God had to fight with, struggle with if you will, Jacob in order to completely break him, both spiritually and physically. Jacob was scared to death on that road to meet his brother, and he was completely alone in the wilderness. He fought with that man for his life. When Jacob wouldn't give up until he received his full blessing, the man gave him his blessing. So now, Jacob would be called Israel. He fought with God, and now God would fight for him.

Dr. Evans put this take on the "what's your name question" a little more current. His paraphrase was, "Jacob, if you are asking me my name, look at your name and you'll know what my name is. And then "Bam!" Jacob got the blessing." Got that, Jacob?

Did simply changing his name change the person? Definitely not. God could not give Jacob his chosen name until God knew Jacob was completely ready and able to receive his blessing. It did not happen overnight, but it did finally happen.

So back to the "what's in a name" question. One of the questions in the study this week talked about what I knew of my own name and my thoughts on it. I struggled with this question at first. I thought to myself "who really cares what my name means?" Yes, it was a perfectly good Bible study mood to be in ... not really.

I penned down some notes after the question. "Erin" means "peace," and according to my baby book, my mom gave me the name because I was born at the end of the Vietnam War, plus my dad was Irish. Sorry Mom, but I hated my name when I was growing up. Perhaps this is a phase little girls go through, but I totally wanted to change my name and not because I was someone famous. Most people spelled my name wrong; some still do. They spelled it "Aaron," and I would always have to say, "No, that's the way boys spell it, and clearly I am not a boy." I even had a high school counselor call out my name during award ceremonies—with, gasp, the whole school watching—and he would pronounce it "Erwin." Seriously, that was not good for an adolescent girl.

My name may mean "peace" but I rarely had it in my life. I was never quite secure in who I was. I struggled to fit in and to find a place to belong—as a child, a teen, and even as an adult. I felt awkward about my weight and my looks, my abilities or lack thereof, choices I made, and so forth. I always had an inner turmoil brewing inside. So unlike Jacob, my name did not reflect who I was out of the womb. I was the complete opposite of peace.

God knows I struggled with Him in the past, but I was always willing to relent, cry "uncle," and walk away. I was not ready to hang on to Him for dear life. However, when I finally had the wrestling match of all wrestling matches with God, I, like Jacob, told God that I was not letting go. Yes, my surrender gave me the promised blessing of salvation, but more importantly, I held on to God because I needed peace.

Did God need to change my name and give me a new name or did He just need me to finally grow into my name? It has not been easy to watch God strip layers away, expose the raw hurt and emotions that were bottled inside, or take away things that seemed important or hard-earned. It has been a long process. It is a process that many have endured and are enduring. I know that the peace that lives within me now, the peace that fills my innermost being is the peace that only comes from the Father, and I believe that I am finally growing into my God-given, grown-up name.

I wrestled with God and we both won. He has me and I have Him.

Peace / Disorder

What about you? Are you living a life that you would define as peaceful? Why or why not?

___

___

___

Is peace something you are craving and praying for right now?

___

___

Are you waiting on a circumstance or someone to change in order to gain peace?

___

___

___

As I listened today to Beth Moore teach her study, *Sacred Secrets,* she said, "Whatever God does, the enemy *tries* to counterfeit" (emphasis mine). We know from God's Word that the enemy is sneaky. He is conniving. He is deceitful, and yes, he thinks he can win, but he cannot. Notice that I emphasized *tries*. Satan *tries* to counterfeit things of God. This is exactly what we are working through in this study. Where the Holy Spirit provides life-giving fruit, the enemy tries to give us dead, rotting fruit and masks it as a failure on our part, a shortcoming, or sin against God. It is all a lie! Satan leads to death, but the Holy Spirit breathes life.

Read Romans 8:6 and complete this sentence.

"So letting your sinful nature control your mind leads to _____. But letting the _____ control your mind leads to _____ and _____."

Who or what is your sinful nature? _____.

Read Ephesians 6:11–12 again:

> Put on the full armor of God, so that you can take your stand against the devil's schemes. For our struggle is not against flesh and blood, but against the rulers, against the authorities, against the powers of this dark world and against the spiritual forces of evil in the heavenly realms.

If you only memorize a handful of scriptures in your lifetime, please make one of them these two verses. When we realize that we are in a constant war, a lot of our life choices, struggles, and issues will begin to make a lot more sense. Augustine said this, "The purpose of all wars is peace." In earthly terms, people go to war against those who are trying to break up the sense of peace. They go to war against people who are trying to invade, rule over them, and oppress them.

Are your current relationships peaceful, are you being ruled over, or are you trying to rule over others?

What happens in relationships when we try and rule over others?

_____

_____

How do you feel when others try and rule over you?

_____

_____

If you are a believer and follower of Jesus Christ, you are engaged in war. There is a war because peace has been sought for you since before you were born. Jesus told his disciples in John 16:33, "I have told you these things, so that in me you may have peace. In this world you will have trouble. But take heart! I have overcome the world." There will be a battle between peace and disorder until Jesus returns.

Great, does this mean I will live in a constant state of disorder? No, friend, no, "For God is not a God of disorder but of peace (1 Corinthians 14:33, NLT). If God is not the God of disorder, but of peace, then who is responsible for disorder? It is you and I and our flesh. It is our open rebellion against God. Before the fall of mankind, Adam and Eve walked peacefully in the garden. They wanted for nothing and were able to walk unclothed, unbothered, and totally cared for. Sin did not exist. However, Eve allowed herself to partake in a conversation with Satan (future note: if Satan tries to talk to you, run! *Do not* listen; resist the devil and he will flee [James 4:7]).

Now the serpent was more crafty than any other beast of the field that the Lord God had made. He said to the woman, "Did God actually say, 'You shall not eat of any tree in the garden'?" And the woman said to the serpent, "We may eat of the fruit of the trees in the garden, but God said, 'You shall not eat of the fruit of the tree that is in the midst of the garden, neither shall you touch it, lest you die.'" But the serpent said to the woman, "You will not surely die. For God knows that when you eat of it your eyes will be opened, and you will be like God, knowing good and evil." So when the woman saw that the tree was good for food, and that it was a delight to the eyes, and that the tree was to be desired to make one wise, she took of its fruit and ate, and she also gave some to her husband who was with her, and he ate. Then the eyes of both were opened, and they knew that they were naked. And they sewed fig leaves together and made themselves loincloths. And they heard the sound of the Lord God walking in the garden in the cool of the day, and the man and his wife hid themselves from the presence of the Lord God among the trees of the garden. But the Lord God called to the man and said to him, "Where are you?" And he said, "I heard the sound of you in the garden, and I was afraid, because I was naked, and I hid myself." He said, "Who told you that you were naked? Have you eaten of the tree of which I commanded you not to eat?" The man said, "The woman whom you gave to be with me, she gave me fruit of the tree, and I ate." Then the Lord God said to the woman, "What is this that you have done?" The woman said, "The serpent deceived me, and I ate."[11]

Peace / Disorder

We have to stop blaming Eve (and Adam) for our sinful nature. We have to stop blaming others for their attitudes and actions toward us. At some point, we have to take ownership of how we react toward others. We have to be the ones who are willing to forgive. We have to be the ones who try and live in peace with others, even if that is extremely difficult during certain seasons and with certain relationships.

"No one can make you feel inferior without your consent." (Eleanor Roosevelt).

As we see in Genesis 3, Satan did his best to break the union between God and mankind. Once he succeeded in that, there was no doubt that the union between Adam and Eve became shaky, and certainly their family was under attack. If you continue reading on in Genesis, you will see that Adam and Eve had two sons, one of whom ended up killing the other. Sin, upon sin, upon sin. We are not privy to all of the conversations that took place between Adam and Eve as they were expelled from the Garden, but if they were anything like some of the conversations that take place in my marriage, they probably were not very kind or forgiving.

If you are married (or if you are not married, think about a family relationship, dating relationship, or friendship), what does it mean to you to be able to forgive your spouse?

_____

_____

How hard is it for you to forgive the little things? For example, your spouse forgot your birthday or anniversary, your spouse showed up late for dinner, or something similar.

_____

_____

Now, what about the things that are a little bigger? For example, your spouse does not care for your friends (which hurts you and limits your ability to spend time with your friends), your spouse spends too much time at the office or enjoying a specific hobby, or your spouse does not communicate with you the way you would like, and so on.

_____

_____

Now, what about the big things? For example, your spouse had an affair, your spouse has a drug or alcohol problem, your spouse cannot seem to keep a job which is causing your family financial burdens, or maybe it is something that your spouse just disclosed to you after years of marriage.

_____

_____

_____

Peace / Disorder

While some things are harder to forgive than others, they need to be forgiven. Sin is sin. If God does not rate our sin and hold us accountable differently for each sin we commit, we cannot hold back forgiveness from others based on our emotions or our rating level either –

> "For whoever keeps the whole law but fails in one point has become accountable for all of it" (James 2:10).

Ruth Bell Graham said, "A happy marriage is the union of two good forgivers." Amen. This is true in marriage and in all of our relationships. We have to be willing to forgive as the Father forgives us. [12]

Prior to God creating order, there was darkness. Genesis 1:2 says, "The earth was without form and void, and darkness was over the face of the deep." God has an order. He created order in His creation. Satan is the being who tried to buck the system and create his own order. Peace comes from God; disorder is the instrument of the enemy. Forgiveness is part of God's order. Unforgiveness is where the disgruntled enemy lives.

It is time you picked whose side you are on in this battle. We cannot continue to have one foot in God's battle while nursing the wounds of our relationships. Let us be people who are willing to extend forgiveness and fully live in the fruit of peace that the Holy Spirit provides. "Make every effort to live in peace with all men and to be holy; without holiness no one will see the Lord" (Hebrews 12:14–15, NIV).

> *Lord, please give me peace. Give me rest. Holy Spirit, I want only the peace that comes from You to live in my heart. Sometimes it may appear that I have it all together, but only You know what lies within my heart. Lord, if my life is in disorder and chaos, reveal to me the root of this problem. Give*

me the strength that only You can give to dig deep and reflect Your love from the depths of my soul. In Jesus' name, Amen.

Week Five

Patience / Impatience

O kay, I am going to start this week off in total disclosure. *I am not a very patient person*! There, I said it. Patience is definitely a fruit that blooms only in certain seasons. I try and blame it on a hormonal imbalance, but that excuse cannot work all the time. More patience is always at the top of my list when I am asking for more of the Holy Spirit.

As I prayed about what to write for this week and as I sought the Spirit's direction on this topic, I felt compelled to address those who are having some issues with God. When we are upset with God, it affects every other relationship we have. When we feel as though God has harmed us, forgotten about us, or failed us, we tend to make hasty decisions and act on our own will instead of His will. We need to be okay with what God allows *and* what He disallows. It may not seem as though we need to forgive God (because seriously, He is the Creator of all things), but we need to be willing to say, "God I am okay with what has transpired. I need to let it go."

The definition of *forgive* is this, "to stop feeling anger toward (someone) or about (something) or to stop blaming (someone)." [13] We can definitely feel anger toward God or blame Him for our problems if we are not careful.

While I do not agree with all of Helen Keller's views, she knew what it could mean to be angry with God. She was born a healthy baby, but at the age of nineteen months, she caught an illness that caused her to go deaf and blind. [14] However, through great persistence, even through her frustrations, she learned how to communicate in a whole new way. She would later say this, "We could never learn to be brave and patient if there were only joy in the world."

What if there were only good things in your life? What if it seemed like God answered every prayer? Do you honestly think you would be happy and grow?

_____

Is there anything you are angry with God about? Is there anything you are trying to blame on Him? Write them out here. Remember, God knows all, so there is really no need to hold anything back.

_____

_____

Let's recall that as believers in Jesus Christ, we are completely forgiven of our sins. Completely! They are not only out of sight, but they are completely blotted out of God's memory. "I am He who blots out your transgressions for My own sake, and I will not remember your sins" (Isa. 43:25).

If God has forgiven us of all the sinful things we have done (and will continue to do), who do we think we are to fail to forgive Him? Further, if we cannot get to a place where we can forgive Him, how can we even begin to expect to forgive others?

How does your anger toward God, at times, affect your relationship with Him?

_____

_____

When you are in a bad place with God, how does that affect every other relationship you have?

_____

_____

Think about a person you are having trouble with, someone with whom you have to spend time or communicate with. Do you have that person in mind? Now, think about how you respond to that person. What is your temperament like? Are you easily frustrated with this person? Angry with this person? Impatient with this person?

_____

Can you remember back to the day you surrendered to Christ? For some, this may have been years ago, and for others of you, it may have been just last week or yesterday. Regardless, can you imagine how patient God was with you? Oh how He waited and waited for some of us to return to Him. Second Peter 3:9 says, "The Lord is not slow to fulfill His promise as some count slowness, but is patient toward you, not wishing that any should perish, but that all should reach repentance." He waited on me and on you, sinners in need of forgiveness. It says He waited patiently. Why? Because He is God the Father, God the Son, and God the Holy Spirit. He bears all of the fruit of the Spirit, and, friends, so can we.

> "The Bible says the fruit of the spirit is longsuffering. I'll tell you one thing about fruit: you will never see a fruit factory. Isn't that right? You see a shirt factory, but you see a fruit orchard. You see, there is no fruit without life. You cannot manufacture patience. The fruit of the Spirit is patience" (Adrian Rogers).

Patience is a heavenly fruit. It is the fruit that allows us to wait and be still among the trials and triumphs of life. It is the fruit that allows us to wait to see how the Lord is going to work something out. His patience is available to us because of His forgiveness.

I do not know about you, but when I am grumpy toward someone, my patience level (which is often low anyway) is running on the reserve. My temper is short. My ability to see that person through grace-filled eyes becomes blurry, and if I am not careful, my Christian love for that person can be drowned out by my inability to forgive that person. Even if that person is God.

Please do not tell me that I am the only person who gets grumpy with God!

Patience / Impatience

Think about a season when you were grumpy with God. Why were you grumpy?

How did that season turn out (if you are already through it)? If you are still in that season, have you been able to see God's hand at work? If so, how?

Before this study, how did you view the word *forgive*? Did you think it could apply to God? Why or why not?

Read Ecclesiastes 7:8.
How do you think patience is related to pride?

Why do you think God asks us to be patient often?

The word for *patience* in the Hebrew text is *'arek,* which is translated as "long, or patient, slow to anger." Where the original word *'arek* occurs in scripture, it is almost always referring to God being "slow to anger." Aren't you happy that God is slow to anger when it comes to you? I know I am.

> "Patience is a grace as difficult as it is necessary, and as hard to come by as it is precious when it is gained" (Charles Spurgeon).

If God is slow to anger with us, don't you think He wants us to be slow to anger towards others? If God is forgiving toward us, don't you think He wants us to be forgiving toward others?

Write out any thoughts you gleaned this week about God being slow to anger toward you and/or your anger and blame toward God.

_____

_____

_____

Last, are there any areas in your life that are lacking patience? How do you think you can resolve this?

_____

_____

Father, you define patience. I am humbled that you are so patient with me. Your patience gives me life and hope. Forgive me when I am lacking in patience, especially as it relates to You and to others. Father, help me see where I am holding unforgiveness from You or from another. Open my eyes and my heart to see how the fruit I am bearing either represent the good, ripe fruit that is from Your Spirit or fruit that is from my own self—from striving, disobedience, unforgiveness. Help me to lead the best life possible here by guiding me with Your Spirit through forgiving others. In Jesus' name, Amen.

Week Six

Kindness – Unkindness

"Write injuries in sand, kindness in marble"
(Author Unknown).

Many of you at one time or another have taken a trip to the beach. A favorite pastime at the beach is to write things in the sand, but inevitably, what happens when you write something in the sand at the beach? The waves come in and wash it completely away. The water does not just sort-of wash it away. No, it is completely erased forever.

The author of this quote above is comparing sand to marble. Anything written in sand will eventually be erased. This is true at the beach and even in a sandbox. However, something etched into marble will last quite a long time, if not forever.

Do you remember the scene in John 8 where the Pharisees brought the woman who had been caught in adultery? Read John 8:3–11.

Kindness – Unkindness

The Pharisees were trying to trap Jesus and cause him to break the law, however, ironically, the Pharisees themselves broke many laws during this encounter. First, they only brought the woman. The Law required that they bring the man, too. Second, they brought no witnesses. The Law required that they bring two witnesses. Third, it was the priest's job to write the laws that were broken and the names of the accused. The priest could do it anywhere, but it had to be a place where it was not permanent. The dust of the temple floor was usually the chosen place. However in this encounter, it was Jesus who ended up writing in the sand because the priest had failed to do so.

What is the significance of the sand? The sand, unlike a permanent surface, gave the accused a chance to repent. The names in the sand could be wiped out, but names written on something permanent could not.

Let's take a look at Jeremiah 17:13. This verse gives us, the readers, context to why the priests were required to write things out.

The exact Hebrew translation is this:

> Oh YHVH, the Immerser (Baptizer) of Israel, all those who leave your way shall be put to shame (publicly embarrassed), those who turn aside from my ways will have their names written in the dust and blotted out, for they have departed from YHVH, the fountain of Mayim Hayim (the waters of life; emphasis mine).

We do not know for sure what Jesus wrote in the sand during his encounter with this woman and the Pharisees. However, we do know that Jesus gave the Pharisees the opportunity to repent of their sins and breaking of the law. He gave them the opportunity to act kindly toward this woman whom they had brought before the council. Instead of repenting and apologizing, however, they ran away from Jesus. The woman's life was spared, and Jesus forgave her of her sin, but we do not ever know what happened to those Pharisees. Did they go home and secretly repent and change their hateful ways? Did they continue to be hateful and legalistic? Did they go home and realize that Jesus was the true Messiah? We have no idea.

There is a beautiful passage of scripture found in Zechariah 3 that creates a perfect picture of forgiveness.

Name the three people in Zechariah 3:1. _____,

_____, and _____.

Who is the one wearing filthy garments?

_____

Do you ever feel like you have been clothed in "filthy garments?"

_____

Who is the one who dresses us in "clean garments?"

_____

In Zechariah 3:3, in addition to putting us in "clean garments," what else does the Lord do for us?

_____

We do not know the actual inscription God inscribed on the stone in Zechariah 3:9, but if we read the whole passage, we see that it says this, "'See, the stone I have set in front of Joshua! There are seven eyes on that one stone, and I will engrave an inscription on it,' says the Lord Almighty, 'and I will remove the sin of this land in a single day.'"

I do not know about you, but I think what could have been inscribed on this stone is the word *forgiven*.

Verse 10 tells us what we do as a result of what is written on that stone: "'In that day each of you will invite your neighbor to sit under your vine and fig tree,' declares the Lord Almighty."

> "Kindness flows from the overflow of the Lord's forgiveness upon us. People who have been deeply graced by God never withhold grace from other people, but people who don't feel like they've been terribly graced are the meanest people on the planet" (Beth Moore).

The things that have caused us pain, grief, sadness, and hurt should be things that we write in the sand so we can forgive as they are washed away from us. We do not want to ever engrave the things that hurt us into stone. We cannot bear that hurt forever. Eventually, the weight of the hurt will crush us just as a gigantic piece of stone would crush us.

Throughout this study, we have been talking a lot about how others hurt us and how we can sometimes get angry and blame God for the things that are happening or have happened to us. But what about the things that we have done that we cannot seem to forgive ourselves for? Perhaps you have made some choices in your life that you wished you had not made. Maybe you have blatantly gone your own way when you knew God was asking you to do something different. Maybe you have even intentionally caused someone pain or harm in order to make yourself look or feel better. You know what? These things are either in the past (yesterday) or still to come in the future (tomorrow). You know who holds the key to all of your burdens? If you said, "Jesus," then you are totally correct.

Jesus wants to carry the burdens of your past, present and future. He wants you only to worry about today. What is He asking you to deal with *today*? What are some of the things you have done that you have been unable to forgive yourself for? Take some time with this. It may not come right in this moment, but meditate on it. I am not asking you to do this to bring up pain, but instead to help you find freedom and peace in the Spirit.

_____

_____

Can you think of ways in which God is trying to use these past experiences to minister to others?

_____

_____

When God places you in a position to see yourself in others, how kind are you to that person or people? For instance, if God has you in a place of ministering to young women who find themselves pregnant outside of marriage, and you, yourself were once in a similar situation or could have been in a similar situation, do you show kindness to these women or do you tend to be more unkind and judgmental?

_____

_____

Why?

_____

_____

The Hebrew word for "kindly" is *chesed*. *Chesed* does not just refer to kindness, but it specifically refers to loyalty and faithfulness.[15] The word *chesed* appears more than two hundred times in the Old Testament alone.

Can you see why kindness is a fruit of the Spirit? If we are *chesed*, we are loyal and faithful. In whom are we loyal and faithful to? Jesus. We are kind because Jesus is kind to us. He intercedes for us, encourages us, walks with us, and forgives us.

But are we *chesed* to ourselves? Some say that "we are our own worst critics." We are hard on ourselves. We beat ourselves up. We can also boast in ourselves and build us up as our own idols if we are not careful, too.

When are you loyal and faithful to yourself? Always? Never? Sometimes? How can you be more loyal and faithful to yourself?

_____

_____

_____

Proverbs 3:3 says, "Never let loyalty and kindness leave you! Tie them around your neck as a reminder. Write them deep within your heart."[16]

The symbol of this gesture is the same as it was back in the day when Moses was talking to the people about the Ten Commandments. In

Deuteronomy 6:8–9, Moses said to the people, "You shall bind them as a sign on your hand and they shall be as frontals on your forehead. You shall write them on the doorposts of your house and on your gates." God already knew we would have short-term memory issues. He knew that we would literally have to inscribe things on garments that we wear or put post-it notes up around our house.

> "Everyone feels benevolent (kind) if nothing happens to be annoying him at the moment" (C.S. Lewis).

What type of events trigger the following from you?
Kindness   Unkindness

_____

_____

What would it take for these events to be moved from the "unkindness" column to the "kindness" column?

_____

_____

Solomon said in Proverbs 11:17, "Your kindness will reward you, but your cruelty will destroy you." And just a couple verses later, in verse 19, he says, "Godly people find life, evil people find death."

We can be cruel to others, but we can also be cruel to ourselves by not allowing ourselves to truly accept the forgiveness that has already been extended as part of a repentant heart. Living in unforgiveness to ourselves can lead us to death. It may not lead us to an eternal separation from Christ (because salvation cannot be lost once given), but it can cause us to walk separately from Christ during this lifetime. He does not choose to walk apart from us, but we can push Him away.

> "Constant kindness can accomplish much. As the sun makes ice melt, kindness causes misunderstanding, mistrust, and hostility to evaporate" (Albert Schweitzer).

Imagine for a minute that every sin you ever committed was displayed for the world to see for a twenty-four-hour period. Everywhere you went, your sins were exposed. If something like this were to happen, how would you react toward the people who cross your path? Would it make you treat people differently? Would it make you be more thankful for the forgiveness you have received because of the gift Jesus gave you?

_____

_____

_____

If like me, you said that you would treat people more kindly and with a more open heart, what do you need to do to start living this way – whether or not your sins are exposed or not?

_____

_____

Friend, you are *forgiven* if you have repented of your sins, turned to Jesus, and received the gift of eternal salvation that has been offered to you. Forgive yourself today. Paul said in Colossians 3 that you are "God's chosen people" and that you are to "clothe yourselves in kindness …" because the Lord forgave you. [17]

Walk in this authority. Walk with kindness tied to your body. If that means wearing something that reminds you to be kind, then so be it. If that means slapping a Jesus fish on the back of your car so you might think about being a nicer driver, so be it. Whatever it takes, walk in the Spirit of kindness to others, and do not be surprised if God puts you in a position to test your kindness by placing you with people who are walking in your forgiven sin. How you respond is a true testament of how forgiven you truly feel.

> *Father, forgive me when I do not forgive myself. Please allow me to walk in the peace of your cleansing. Thank you, Father, that my sins have been completely forgiven and have been erased in the sand. Thank you for giving me the opportunity to repent and turn to You. May Your grace be the constant that guides my life. May Your grace be reflected in how I treat others. May my kindness remind me of the loyalty and faithfulness that You have for me and that I have for You. In Jesus' name, Amen.*

Week Seven

Goodness – Evil

T his week is good, y'all. It is good because it is all about God, and He is good!

"Give thanks to the LORD, for he is *good*, for his steadfast love endures forever" (Psalm 136:1, *emphasis mine*).

Why does it matter if God is good?

_____

_____

Billy Graham, the great evangelist, said this, "Man has two great spiritual needs. One is for forgiveness. The other is for goodness." These two things are found in God, the Creator. From the beginning of creation, as early as verse 4 in the Book of Genesis, we are presented with the concept of "good" from God's perspective. Each day as creation unfolded, we see that "God saw that it was good."

The word for "good" in the Hebrew form is *towb*. Depending upon the context, this word is translated in the King James Version as "goodness, precious, better, well, beautiful, favour, and fine."[18] God is *towb,* and because we are made in His image, we are *towb* in His sight, too. Claim that today!

I love Billy Graham's quote because it is so simple. The two things he mentioned, forgiveness and goodness, are truly all that we need. From the moment sin entered the world, we needed the opportunity for God to forgive us. Without this forgiveness, we are eternally separated from Him. We also need goodness because we need God and He is good. I love that the Holy Spirit affords us the opportunity to walk in the fruit of goodness. I love that even on my worst days, I am clothed in his righteousness and walk in His goodness.

Do you truly believe you are good?

_____

Read Genesis 1:27. Do you truly believe that you are made in His image?

_____

_____

If you are hesitant to answer, "Yes," what is holding you back?

_____

_____

As I watched the news this week and watched the pictures unfold on the television screen, I was reminded just how much evil there is in the world. The pictures were so very somber as the black hearses traveled down the highway in the Netherlands. Bodies were in those hearses—a couple hundred bodies to be exact. One moment, some of these people were expectant about holiday plans in Malaysia. The next, the plane and the people in it were intentionally shot out of the sky over Ukraine. There are no words when innocent people are killed during times of war, and this incident is especially heinous because this commercial plane was merely flying in the air space over two war-torn countries. My soul hurts for the people affected by this tragedy. Things like this bring a new realness to evil in the world. What if it happened to be my husband on that plane flying overseas as part of his business? Would I be able to forgive those people who orchestrated that attack? Will those touched by this tragic event be able to forgive? One of the villager women who was interviewed after this event said, "I didn't go to the crash site. My soul cannot stand it." [19] Honestly, whose soul can?

There is a Tibetan proverb that says, "Goodness speaks in a whisper, evil shouts." Isn't that the truth? The everyday "goodness" of life goes virtually unnoticed. Sure, we randomly hear about some acts of kindness, but usually it is the "evil" events that get the most press coverage. Why? Because Satan is insecure! He needs to shout so people will hear him. He has a larger-than-life inferiority complex. God is good and in control and like an idyllic momma, He can whisper and get the world to hear.

Here in the United States, we had our own horrific act of terrorism. The morning of September 11, 2001, has forever changed America. We know the feeling of innocent people going about their daily business one moment and tragically torn apart in the next. I do not know about you, but I remember the exact moment when I realized what was happening. Fear, uncertainty, anger, confusion, and grief enveloped me, all at the same time. I was four months pregnant with my first child, highly hormonal and confused as to why I was bringing a child into such a scary world. Again, I was confronted with the question, "what if it had been my husband in one of the buildings?" He had, in fact, been in one of those buildings just a few days prior to this horrific event. Would I have been able to forgive the terrorists? Would I have been able to forgive those who had given orders to stay put in a building that no one would have ever imagined could have crumpled like that?

There is a scripture that many do not like to hear during times of extreme grief. It is sometimes misquoted and misused, but its meaning can bring great comfort to those who walk in the fruit of goodness. Romans 8:28 says, "And we know that for those who love God all things work together for good, for those who are called according to His purpose." This verse does not mean that only good things will happen to people. It does not mean that everything makes sense to us or works out the way we think is good. No, it means that good is what is good according to God. Our finite minds have a hard time understanding an infinite God. If we are not careful, our limited ability and our attempts to try and figure out God can lead us onto the path of unforgiveness and anger, which ultimately leads us to be on team "evil."

What do I mean by this?

If you were a citizen of the United States on September 11, 2001, how did the events that unfolded affect your views on terrorists?

_____

_____

_____

Because these terrorists were Middle Eastern in nature, does that fact alone cause you to believe that every person of Middle-eastern descent is a potential threat?

_____

_____

If so, is this because you have fear or is it because you have anger or unforgiveness (yes, you can have unforgiveness because this event has caused so many things in our country to be different)?

_____

_____

Are fear, anger, and unforgiveness hindering your ability to be a witness for Jesus Christ to this people group?

_____

_____

Now, let's apply this scenario to something or someone else in your life that is a little closer to home. Can you think of someone or something that is causing you fear or anger? If so, is there unforgiveness that is causing a hindrance to being the best possible witness for Jesus Christ to that person or in general?

_____

Romans 12:9 says, "Let love be genuine. Abhor what is evil; hold fast to what is good." Our love for one another cannot be genuine if we are living in a state of unforgiveness. If I am unable to forgive someone, I cannot love him or her with my whole heart because a part of my heart is filled with unforgiveness. Jesus commands us to "love one another" as the second greatest commandment. [20] It really is not an option for the believer.

God is good, and He has so many good things stored up for those who love and fear Him. [21]

Many of us are not walking around with wounds that are visible. Many of us are not walking around trying to forgive those whom the world knows about. However, most of us, according to A.W. Tozer, are "wounded souls." Forgiveness requires humility, and yet far too often, we are too proud. Proverbs 21:4 warns us against being proud, "Haughty eyes, a proud heart, and evil actions are all sin." I do not know about you, but my proud heart is full of sin at times, and to have my proud heart and evil actions all lined up in the same sentence as sin, makes me tremble a bit. I do not want to be remembered as being proud, unforgiving, or evil. I want to be remembered as being humble, forgiving, and worthy of walking in my calling. I want to be transformed daily into being more and more like Christ.

> "Oh, taste and see that the Lord is good! Blessed is the man
> who takes refuge in Him" (Psalm 34:8)!

Friends, God is calling you to forgiveness because He wants you to walk in the fruit of goodness. He is good, and He wants you to be good, perfect, and highly favored.

If there is anything holding you back from this goodness, please write it in the margin.

Give it to the Lord. Extend forgiveness. Repent of pride. Whatever God is calling you to, do it today. Claim the goodness that He has stored up for you and so badly wants to give to you.

Father God, the Great I Am, Yahweh, Elohim, and the All-Sufficient One, You are so good, perfect, and holy. Thank You for creating us in Your image and giving us the possibility of Your goodness. Thank You for storing up Your goodness for each one of us. Father, today, in this moment, I pray for each person reading this that they would release whatever unforgiveness is holding them back from receiving the immense treasures of goodness upon them that You would give them. Lord, for we know that when goodness flows from us, there is no mistaking that we are children of God. Lord, let no evil take hold in me today. Father, work out my past mistakes, my past choices, my unforgiveness—any part of my testimony that You need—for Your good and for Your name's sake. Thank You for allowing me to take part in Your Kingdom work. In Jesus' name, Amen.

Week Eight

Faithfulness – Disloyalty

When you think of the word *faithful*, what is the first thing that pops into your mind?

Perhaps because we are in a Bible study, your first thought was God. That would be the good Christian answer! But oftentimes when I am thinking of faithfulness, my thoughts turn toward marriage. We are called to be "faithful" spouses.

So what does *faithful* really mean? The Greek word for "faithful" is *pistos*.[22] It is defined as "trust, worthy of trust, to be relied upon." The Hebrew word for "faithful" is *'aman*.[23] It states that while *faithful* means to be trustworthy, it also paints a picture of someone who supports, upholds, and nourishes.

Is there no wonder why we declare God as the almighty, faithful One? He certainly supports each one of us, upholds us, and nourishes us each and every day. I do not know about you, but there is not one person, not even my faithful husband, who does all these things each and every single day.

Faithfulness – Disloyalty

There is only God who does all these things and more. He truly is faithful and worthy of our trust.

Here is some freeing information for some of you. God is faithful no matter what you or I do. Did you hear that? He is faithful even when we are not. His Word tells us in Hebrews 13:8 that He is "the same yesterday and today and forever." He does not change.

This week is going to get a little tough. I mean, it is going to be tough because we are going to be talking about you. I hope and pray that you hang in here with me. I hope by the end of this week, you feel like you have been through one of those celebrity cleanses and have lost a ton of weight—spiritual weight, that is. Let's discuss why.

2 Timothy 2:13 says, "If we are faithless, He remains faithful—for He cannot deny Himself." The word for faithless here is the Greek word *apisteō* and it means "to betray a trust, be unfaithful or to have no belief." [24] Paul was just reconfirming that God is faithful, and He does not go against His word.

You know what? We do. Why? Because we have a sin nature.

I do not know about you, but it has taken me years to forgive myself for some of the choices I made during my prodigal years. I carried so much weight around that it began to take a toll on me. These are some of the layers of unforgiveness of myself I carried around:

Shame
Guilt
Regret
Fear
Embarrassment
Frustration

I grew up going to church, but I did not really "get it." Honestly, if someone had asked me when I was in my early twenties whether or not

God would let me into Heaven, I would not have known how to respond. I mean, I was not without sin for sure, and I had no idea what the correct answer was. I had a lot of "not-so-good" works—that was for sure.

List some of the not-so-good "spiritual weight" you are carrying around with you right now.

_____

_____

Why are you still carrying it around?

_____

_____

If I look at 2 Timothy 2:13 again and put my own name in there, I have to admit, I was quite faithless for many years. I was unfaithful to God because I failed to fear Him and I failed to have faith in Him. My ears and heart were completely closed to His covenant promise for His people.
Read Isaiah 40:2.

How do these words spoken by the prophet Isaiah speak to your heart even today?

_____

Faithfulness – Disloyalty

What does it mean that the Lord gave "double" or "punished twice" (depending on your translation)?

_____

_____

Does this extreme punishment frighten you or give you great peace?

_____

_____

If it frightens you, let's clear up what the prophet Isaiah was prophesying about. Isaiah was prophesying about the Good News of God's salvation. He was telling the people of Jerusalem that the Lord was coming to rescue His own. Hallelujah!

The "double" or "twice over" punishment refers to the full brunt of God's wrath. Who suffered the full brunt of God's wrath for all sinners past, present, and future?

_____

_____

I am hoping everyone answered *Jesus!*

Even to this day, God is faithful. Over two thousand years ago, God sent His one and only Son to this earth to be born as a baby and to die on a cross for all of us. Why? Because God loves you, me, and all of us that much.

> For God so loved the world, that He gave His only Son, that whoever believes in Him should not perish but have eternal life (John 3:16).

I know He wants you to love yourself that much, too.

I was disloyal to God because I sinned against Him, yes, but I was so much more disloyal to God because I disbelieved that He could love a sinner like me. The choices of my sin were nothing compared to the fact that I failed to acknowledge Him and failed to acknowledge the gift that He was so desperately trying to give me.

Read Ephesians 2:8–9.

In your own words, define grace.

_____

_____

Grace in the Greek form is *charis*. One of the definitions of this word says, "of the merciful kindness by which God, exerting his holy influence upon souls, turns them to Christ, keeps, strengthens, increases them in Christian faith, knowledge, affection, and kindles them to the exercise of the Christian virtues."[25] Grace is that thing that pursues you in the middle of your mess. Grace is the thing that pursues you in the darkness, and it is grace that calls you out of that darkness into His wonderful Light.

It is His grace that increases your faith. It is also His grace that gives you the ability to forgive yourself as He has forgiven you.

> "Sometimes the most difficult person to pardon is oneself, but forgiveness is never complete until that has happened" (Charles F. Stanley).

One might look at Charles Stanley's statement and say *Whoa! Wait a minute. Forgiveness is complete the minute one accepts Christ as their Savior.* Yes, while salvation and forgiveness are granted the minute someone accepts Christ as their Savior, I think Charles Stanley's statement is totally true.

Jesus does forgive us immediately at the moment of salvation. Our sins are "blotted out."[26] But while He may forgive us, we do not always forgive ourselves right away. Why?

We are babies at the moment of salvation. First Peter 2:2 says, "Like newborn infants, long for the pure spiritual milk, that by it you may grow up into salvation." Often times, the reality of His work on the Cross does not immediately sink in. The reality that He chooses to pursue you among the millions in this world does not quite register, and oftentimes when it does start to sink in that He loves you that much, that He has forgiven you, the devil will try and come in and steal your joy. The devil will try and come in steal away the gift of forgiveness and convince you that it is all a lie.

Ephesians 6 warns us that we are in a spiritual battle against the devil and all of his schemes. We have to be equipped through God's Word to do battle against the spiritual realm. The moment you decide to respond to God by faith and accept Jesus as your Lord and Savior, you become a direct enemy of Satan. Let me assure you, Satan is not happy about the roster change.

> "God's guilt brings enough regret to change us. Satan's guilt, on the other hand, brings enough regret to enslave us" (Max Lucado).

Satan is the ruler of disloyalty and unfaithfulness. He wanted to become equal to God, and as a result, God pushed him out of Heaven (*see* Isaiah 14:12–15 and Ezekiel 28:12–15). Satan will tempt us into thinking things that are not quite exactly the way God says they are. He did it with Adam and Eve in the Garden, and you better bet he will try to do it with you and me.

Choose today that you will be on God's team, not Satan's. Choose to believe God's promises of rescue, salvation, and total forgiveness of your sins. Choose to believe in His total faithfulness to His people. Choose today to forgive yourself of any past or present sins.

Take a minute and seek God. Ask Him to reveal the sins that you are having a hard time forgiving yourself for. Ask Him to reveal to you why it is that you cannot let these things go. Ask Him to increase your faithfulness. After you have spent some time with Him, write down what He told you.

_____

_____

Were any of the things you just wrote the same as when we first started this section?

_____

_____

If not, what changed?

_____

Faithfulness – Disloyalty

According to Hebrews 4:13, "Nothing in all creation is hidden from God. Everything is naked and exposed before his eyes."

Shortly after surrendering myself to Christ and finally acknowledging Him as my Lord and Savior, I had a vision, a dream, if you will. I did not know scripture at all at that point, and God was so patient in giving me "spiritual milk." In this vision, I was naked and exposed in many ways. Even then, I did not understand the dream completely. It has taken years in His Word to find the truths that help what He delivers make sense. However, in that moment during that vision when Satan was trying to dump all my junk back into my life and heap on layers of shame, guilt, and regret, I was adamant that Satan was not going to be allowed to do that. As I did battle with Satan, God gave me the following word, "The fear of the Lord is the beginning of wisdom." I did not know at the time that this saying was found several times in the Book of Proverbs and in the Psalms, but God knew I needed that word at that moment.

I feared Him because of His grace and forgiveness for me. I feared Him because of the sacrifice of His son. I feared Him because He rescued me. I feared Him because of His awesomeness. "Oh what joy for those whose disobedience is forgiven, whose sin is put out of sight" (Psalm 32:1). If He can forgive us, then we should be faithful to Him by extending forgiveness to ourselves. May you never live another moment in unforgiveness of yourself. Be joyful and thankful for all that He has given you.

In Psalm 103, David wrote an acrostic poem with one verse for each letter of the Hebrew alphabet. It is a beautiful poem that celebrates God's goodness, faithfulness, forgiveness, compassion, and desire for us to remain faithful and loyal to Him, as He is loyal and faithful to His children and His promises.

> Let all that I am praise the LORD; with my whole heart, I will praise his holy name. Let all that I am praise the LORD;

may I never forget the good things he does for me. He forgives all my sins and heals all my diseases. He redeems me from death and crowns me with love and tender mercies. He fills my life with good things. My youth is renewed like the eagle's! The LORD gives righteousness and justice to all who are treated unfairly. He revealed his character to Moses and his deeds to the people of Israel. The LORD is compassionate and merciful, slow to get angry and filled with unfailing love. He will not constantly accuse us, nor remain angry forever. He does not punish us for all our sins; he does not deal harshly with us, as we deserve. For his unfailing love toward those who fear him is as great as the height of the heavens above the earth. He has removed our sins as far from us as the east is from the west. The LORD is like a father to his children, tender and compassionate to those who fear him. For he knows how weak we are; he remembers we are only dust (Ps. 103:1–14 NLT).

If God can forgive us and completely erase our sins, we need to do the same. If we do not, we cannot fully walk in all the attributes of the fruit of the Spirit that He is trying to offer us. Faithfulness and disloyalty cannot grow on the same vine. One will always choke out the other.

Which one will it be for you?

> *Father, You are Yĕhovah. There is none like You. There will never be anyone like You. You set everything into motion. You see my sins, and even still, You love me. You sent Your Son to die for my sins. He took my place. Because of His death, which bore the full brunt of Your wrath for mankind, I have life. Father, forgive me when I have little faith to believe Your love*

is so big. Forgive me for not forgiving myself. Forgive me for running away from You in shame and guilt. Forgive me for allowing myself to be a slave to Satan and this world. Thank You, Father, for redeeming me through Your grace. Thank You for this gift of eternal life. Father, I pray for those who do not yet know or understand the gift of Your saving grace. I pray Father that many would receive Your gift so that their sins may be forgiven once and for all. In Jesus' name, Amen.

Week Nine

Gentleness / Abruptness

There is nothing I like better than a gentle wind on a stifling, hot day. Why? Because it brings relief to a tough situation. A gentle breeze can cool me off and move the still, hot, sticky, and stagnant air around me. The same can be said of a gentle spirit, the gentle spirit of the Holy Spirit living within each believer in Jesus Christ.

> "Our identity rests in God's relentless tenderness for us revealed in Jesus Christ" (Brennan Manning).

Jesus is gentle with us. He takes time with us. He goes out of His way for us. He forgives us without asking for much in return.

Jesus' gentle spirit is revealed to us in the encounter Jesus had with the Samaritan woman at the well. This encounter, found in John 4, reveals so much to us about God's desire to call all to Himself—even those who are shunned, lonely, seemingly unforgivable or unloved, and those currently living in blatant sin.

Gentleness / Abruptness

Jesus and his disciples had just left Jerusalem and instead of going around Samaria, like most of the religious people would have done, Jesus went directly through Samaria. After coming upon Jacob's Well located just outside the town of Sychar, Jesus sat down at the well and took a rest. His disciples went on ahead the remaining half-mile to a mile to find food for the group.

At this well in the middle of the daytime heat, a woman came to draw water. Scripture tells us that when this woman came to the well, Jesus asked her to fetch him some water. This was not typical of that day for many reasons. For starters, this woman was ... well a woman. Men, especially rabbis, would not speak to a woman in public. A respectable woman would have fled the minute a man spoke to her. Second, this woman was a Samaritan. The Jewish people had a four hundred year hatred for the Samaritan people. The Samaritans claimed to worship the one true God, followed the first five books of the Old Testament (the Pentateuch), and followed many Jewish traditions. However, because the Samaritans were of mixed blood—Jewish and pagan—the Jewish people thought of them as "dogs" and unclean. Finally, because Jesus asked this woman to give him water, had he actually drunk the water she drew for him, he would have made himself ceremoniously unclean.

Jesus, in his gentle spirit, did not seem bothered by any of it. When Jesus asked her for some water, it says in verse 7 that she was shocked and began to run down all the reasons why he should not be asking her for water. Are there times you feel shocked that Jesus takes time with you even if it means it might make him unclean by being in your presence?

I hope the list was not very long! If it was, take heart: Jesus is not affected by the rules that man imposes. He does not mind spending time with all of us because if we get right down to it, we are all sinners. Romans 3:23 says, "For all have sinned and fall short of the Glory of God."

Even in her self-doubt, Jesus kept gently pursuing this woman. Even in the moment when it seems like Jesus is about to lay the hammer down, he did not. Jesus said to the woman in verse 16, "Go and get your husband."

Uh oh.

This woman had a choice to make at that moment. She could have either said, "Okay" and just took off running for home or she could have confessed that she did not have a husband. Perhaps because of Jesus' gentleness and the tenderness in which he spoke with her, she chose the latter. She told Jesus that she did not have a husband. Jesus, of course, knew she did not have a husband, and in fact, this woman had had five husbands and was currently living with a man who was not her husband. Jesus kept pressing in and called her out. Here was this poor woman who had already been shunned by the people of her village and now, a total stranger, was calling her out on her sin as well.

Have you ever felt like when it rains it pours? Has there been a time in your life, perhaps in your current situation, where someone knows something about you and wants you to talk about it?

_____

_____

_____

If so, how does this person approach you? In what manner? Are they gentle, condescending, judgmental, unforgiving, or loving?

___

___

___

In a seven-sentence exchange with Jesus, this woman was given the opportunity to unload her shame, her sorrow, her hurt, her disappointment, and her loneliness on the person of Jesus Christ. He met her at the well that day to forgive her of her sins and to give her hope. When this woman left Jesus and her water pot at the well, he did not even say anything about forgiveness or even changing her ways. He said, "Now go and preach what I have told you." It was simply her acknowledgment of Jesus as the Messiah that lifted those burdens from her and changed her immediately.

What would have happened if this woman had not allowed Jesus' gentle spirit and words to be received as blessings?

___

___

If you read on further in John 4, what happens once the woman returns to her village?

___

___

How do you think it is that a woman who had been completely shunned by her own people to the point of not even being able to do a daily mundane task in the presence of other women, is listened to upon her arrival back in town?

_____

_____

_____

What happens to our spirits when we truly acknowledge the truth that we are completely forgiven?

_____

_____

_____

We learn that when this woman returned to her village, she told everyone about meeting the Messiah. The scriptures tell us that people believed her, and because of her testimony, many were saved.[27] Scripture tells us further that she even acknowledged her sin publicly because she said, "He told me of everything I had done."[28] I can picture clearly the women and men shaking their heads as if to say, "Hmmm … .hmmmm … that's right." She did not care at that moment what they thought because her spirit had been changed. The moment she encountered the living Christ, the living water, her demeanor shifted. She was no longer a shunned woman. No, she was a sinner forgiven by Christ Himself.

Gentleness / Abruptness

What might the reactions of the people been had this woman returned to town with an abrupt, accusatory tone instead of a joyful spirit?

_____

_____

_____

This woman, in the world's eyes, had every right to go back and accuse her accusers. She could have said something like, "You all shunned me, condemned me, hated me, spit on me, and talked about me," but she did not. On the half-mile to mile journey back to town, she allowed the thought of her being forgiven settle into her soul, and as a result, she was able to forgive all of those who disliked her. As she forgave, the burden of sharing the Messiah with everyone far outweighed anything else.

Are you still in the process of trying to understand that Jesus really has forgiven *all* of your sins?

_____

_____

Are you in the half-mile to mile journey where forgiving others is being stripped from your soul? If so, what is on your heart to share with them?

_____

_____

What have you done as a result of the forgiveness of your Savior?

_____

_____

> "Gentleness is not apathy but is an aggressive expression of how we view people. We see people as so valuable that we deal with them in gentleness, fearing the slightest damage to one for whom Christ died. To be apathetic is to turn people over to mean and destructive elements, to truly love people cause for us to be aggressively gentle" (Gayle D. Erwin).

Admittedly, I struggle sometimes with the fact that Jesus really does forgive all of my sins and transgressions. The enemy would always like me to believe that it is not possible. It is at those times that I must rely on the Word of God to believe with all my heart that what He says is Truth.

I believe God sometimes needs me to pause in my writing because He needs to be the one giving me material. This week's lesson, for some reason, has been slow to come. That is, until God sent me the perfect life example just the other day.

> Brothers, if anyone is caught in any transgression, you who are spiritual should restore him in a spirit of gentleness. Keep watch on yourself, lest you too be tempted (Galatians 6:1, NLT).

We have been in our current home for the past ten years. About seven years ago, I met a man who made me pause and think. One day as I was walking past my laundry room door, I happened to look outside and saw a man, kind of a scruffy looking man, bending down and extending his hand through my electric gate. He was talking to my beagle and patting him on the head. This beagle of mine howled at everyone who came near or on our property. However, this time, my beagle was just sitting there calmly with a stranger. I approached this man to figure out why he was there. It turned out that while he was not technically homeless, he was renting a room at an inn, and he was looking for work. His name was Marx. He was a window washer, and he wanted to know if he could wash our windows for some money. It was the middle of the day, and I was home with my children, but I felt okay since he passed my beagle test. (Please know that I do not advise anyone just to let perfect strangers onto their property!) I fed him, he washed the windows, I paid him, and he left.

Honestly, it was a strange time in my life, and I was so fearful of things that I believed God had sent this man to get me over my fear of fear because when he was done, he just sort of vanished. I almost thought he was an angel! However, he was not an angel, and I saw him periodically in my neighborhood throughout the years. A few years after he initially washed my windows, he knocked at the front door and asked if he could wash my windows again. It was not an ideal time that day, but he promised that if I would give him money that day, he would return the next day to wash the windows. I gave him the money, but he did not show up the next day. Even after this, I would still see him in the neighborhood, and I found out later that he had come back to the house again a couple times, but my husband was the one to answer the door.

Last week as I was leaving to run some errands, there was Marx again. This time, he approached me in the middle of the street as I sat in my car, approaching the stop sign. I lowered my window and smiled at him. The first words out of his mouth were "I know a few years back I got some money from you and never showed up to clean your windows ... there is no excuse."

He went on to say many other words. Because I needed my windows cleaned again, I let him start cleaning them, telling him that I would be back in an hour and a half to pay him. As I pulled up to my house, there he was, sitting on my porch waiting for me to return so he could get started on the back windows. As I exited my car, he said, "I am just so thankful that you chose to forgive me today." These words may not seem like much to you, but to a woman who is writing a Bible study on forgiveness, they are like food for the soul.

I let him in the back yard and went inside to make him a couple sandwiches. As I prepared to go outside, I felt the gentle nudge of the Holy Spirit tell me to print off this Bible study for him and give him a copy.

It turns out that Marx's father has been a pastor for the past sixty-five years. Marx, admittedly, is fighting his own demons and said that but for a father who fights for him on his knees, he would have no chance. We talked some theology (he can quote KJV scripture like nobody's business), and I let him finish up. As he got ready to leave he said, "I'm going to go and forgive someone today who has wronged me. You've reminded me of that."

I have no idea where that forgiveness will go or what it will mean, but I know that God does. I know that God ordained our divine appointment that day.

I also know that I could have gotten in God's way that day. I could have ignored Marx and just waved as I approached the stop sign. I could have been abrupt and confronted him about the fact that he basically stole money from me. I did not do any of those things, and I can say it is only because of the Holy Spirit's gentleness living in me that I reacted the way I did. The Holy Spirit needed to have a conversation with Marx that day, and He used me as His vessel.

My husband and I had the opportunity to spend a few days at the Billy Graham Training Center at The Cove in North Carolina this week. It was a birthday present from my husband, and our pastor happened to be the

Gentleness / Abruptness

one teaching this week. He taught on the Days of Elijah found in 1 Kings 17–19. As I listened to him teach on our last day, God's gentle Spirit jumped off the page.

Read 1 Kings 17–19.

Elijah had been bold when he confronted King Ahab. He challenged the king to a showdown on the mountain. God prevailed on that mountain, and Elijah was on a spiritual high. However, when the evil Jezebel heard what had taken place, she told Elijah that she was going to kill him within twenty-four hours. Elijah's boldness turned to fear, and he ran and hid under a tree and prayed to God that he would die. Duh ... had he stayed put, he could have been dead in twenty-four hours. As our pastor pointed out, Elijah did not really want to die; he wanted to live.

What happened in 1 Kings 19:5–8?

_____

_____

_____

Read on further in verses 9–10.
Why do you think the Lord asked Elijah what he was doing there?

_____

_____

Elijah at that moment was not remorseful for his running away. He was not humble in the presence of the Lord. In fact, he confronted the Lord as if the Lord had not taken care of him and that Elijah was the one and only person working for the Lord.

Think about someone you are dealing with right now, perhaps someone you have engaged in a similar conversation. How do you respond when someone fails to be repentant for an act or word against you?

_____

_____

We know how God reacted in this particular case. Verse 12 says that God appeared in a "low whisper." Some translations say "gentle whisper." God gently asked Elijah again what he was doing. Elijah again answered with pride and self-pity. God made the next move and gave Elijah further instructions.

Let's notice, just like Jesus with the woman at the well, God did not outwardly chastise Elijah. Instead, God just kept pressing in and giving him further instruction so that Elijah could continue to be used by God.

> "It is wonderful how attractive a gentle, pleasant manner is, and how much it wins hearts" (Francis de Sales).

We should all react this way more. Remember, forgiving someone does not make them right; it makes you free. We do not always have to get a word in, be proven right, or force someone to seek our forgiveness. By gently responding to them, oftentimes, their convictions will kick in and things can move forward. We are not responsible for forcing someone to be repentant, but we are responsible for living in a state of unforgiveness. We cannot control another person, but we can learn to allow the Spirit to control our responses.

God did not specifically mention forgiving Elijah. He recommissioned him. Jesus did not specifically tell the woman at the well that she was forgiven. He sent her on her way and told her to tell others what he had said. I never specifically told Marx that I forgave him for taking my money. In each circumstance, it was the gentle response of the one extending forgiveness that provided the forgiveness.

God forgives gently. Jesus forgives gently. The fruit of the Spirit is gentleness. We can be gentle and forgiving through the power of the Holy Spirit within us. Be encouraged. If the Lord is asking you to respond in gentleness, He will give you the words. Just ask Him.

> *Lord God, You are so faithful in always pursuing us for Your purposes. Lord, may I allow Your Holy Spirit to fill me to overflowing today and every day so that the Spirit can be more present in me than I am in myself. Lord Jesus, help me to be gentle just like You. Help me to respond to others through a spirit of gentleness so that we ... both them and me ... can continue to walk in the calling You have placed on our lives. Lord Jesus, show me who it is that I am being abrupt to and gently rebuke my heart. Forgive me, Jesus, when I am abrupt and cause others to stumble. Encourage my heart today through Your Word that lives in and through me. In Jesus' name, Amen.*

Week Ten

Self-Control / Rashness

Oh how many times I say "self-control" in a week. I have younger children so this applies to much of what they do (or do not do) and much of what I say. In all reality, self-control is something most of us struggle with throughout our entire lives. However, there is a difference between worldly self-control and biblical self-control.

Webster's dictionary defines *self-control* as, "restraint exercised over one's own impulses, emotions or desires." While this definition may seem good, it is not entirely correct. We have a hard time exercising control over our own actions in our own strength. This is where the Holy Spirit helps us.

The Greek word for "self-control" is *egkráteia*. It means, "dominion within proceeding out from within oneself, but not by oneself." So for the believer, self-control can only be accomplished by the power of the Lord.[29] Returning back to our lists of the fruit of the Spirit found in Galatians 5:22–23, we see that self-control is the final fruit listed. I love all the more that the biblical definition of self-control says we cannot do it alone. We need the Holy Spirit in all aspects of our lives.

Self-Control / Rashness

Friends, we have been together now for nine weeks, walking through the nine attributes of the fruit of the Spirit and how they look through the lens of a person who has extended or can extend forgiveness, as well as through the lens of someone who may still be walking through unforgiveness. My desire is that by the end of this chapter, you will without a doubt know if you are truly walking around totally aware of the Father's forgiveness for you, as well as truly knowing that you have been able to forgive all of those who have in some way put you in a position of having to forgive them, including your own self.

> "Self-control is the exercise of inner strength under the direction of sound judgment that enables us to do, think, and say the things that are pleasing to God" (Jerry Bridges).

Years ago as I was planning my wedding, I received a letter in the mail from my stepfather's mother. She is a Christian, and she decided that she needed to let me know how displeased she was that I was not allowing my stepfather to walk me down the aisle on my wedding day. Now, I am not totally sure if she took this all to the Lord in prayer before she contacted me, but without even fully realizing it, I had caused her to be angry with me. I applaud her for not letting this anger eat away at her, but I still question whether or not she is truly free from this situation. You see, in her letter she wrote these words to me, "Because I am a Christian, I will forgive you, but I will not forget." Words are powerful. It does not matter if the words are written or spoken. Either way they can build up, tear down, or destroy.

The Hebrew word for "rashness" is *bata' or batah*. It means "to speak angrily or thoughtlessly."[30]

Proverbs 12:18 illustrates the difference between rash words and good words, "There is one whose rash words are like sword thrusts, but the tongue of the wise brings healing." The words written by my grandmother in that letter definitely did not bring healing to an already tense situation. I would have actually felt better about the whole ordeal had she written about her anger alone without throwing in the forgiveness part. I do not believe she was wholeheartedly forgiving out of the overflow of her heart, but rather because she felt as though she *had* to forgive me "because she was a Christian."

Sometimes that is the exact place we get stuck. We get stuck in the "I *have* to forgive mode" instead of "I am *going* to forgive mode." It is all about the heart. We cannot forgive in our own strength. The self-control it takes to speak kind, loving words of forgiveness to someone does not come from ourselves but from someone in addition to us. We mentioned Jesus' conversation earlier in this study about the fact that He must leave so His Father could send a "Helper" and an "Advocate" for us (John 14:15). He knew we would be able to do nothing in our strength that looked anything Christ-like.

Do you think that God *had* to send His Son to die for each one of us, or do you think He did it out of the overflow of His heart?

_____

_____

_____

Next to each of these actions, write down how you feel when someone does the following to you:

Violates you _____

Says an unkind word _____

Self-Control / Rashness

Betrays your trust _____

Steals from you _____

Hurts a loved one _____

What is usually your first response when something like what was mentioned above happens?

_____

_____

_____

This is what God's response to us is – "Even before He made the world, God *loved* us and *chose* us in Christ to be holy and without fault in His eyes. God *decided in advance* to adopt us into His own family by bringing us to Himself through Jesus Christ. This is what He *wanted* to do, and it gave Him great pleasure."[31]

God knew us before we even knew Him. Before we accepted Jesus as our Savior (if in fact you have accepted Him as your personal Lord and Savior), He knew all of our sins. He knew all of the things that violated Him and His Word. Yet, He still chose to *fully* forgive each one of us who are believers in Jesus Christ. He did not *have* to. He *chose* to. We have to be willing to make those same choices as we surrender to Him and operate in the Spirit as opposed to operating in the rash spirit of self.

> "Don't do something permanently stupid because you are temporarily upset" (Toby Mac).

What happens when you allow yourself a "cooling off period" or take it to the Lord in prayer before responding?

_____

_____

> "We must have a spirit of power towards the enemy, a spirit of love towards men, and a spirit of self-control towards ourselves" (Watchman Nee).

Jesus loved to teach in parables. They were examples that people could understand. In Matthew 18, we see Jesus present the parable of the unforgiving debtor. Jesus' disciple, Peter, had a good question. Peter asked Jesus in verse 21, "Lord, how often should I forgive someone who sins against me? Seven times?"

How many times did Jesus say Peter needed to forgive someone who sins against him?

_____

If we read further in that passage in verses 23–25, would you say that the king acted in a self-controlled manner or a bit rash?

_____

What did the king do to the servant who owed him money?

_____

Self-Control / Rashness

Aren't you glad that debt collectors do not have the power to do this to most of us today! Somehow the master had a change of heart and felt pity for the servant after the servant cried at his feet for mercy. Does this image remind you of someone else?

_____

_____

Once the king forgave the servant's debt, the servant went and did something a little rash. What did the servant go and do?

_____

_____

This servant, who was owed a debt by a fellow servant, refused to find pity on him and forgive him and threw this servant in jail. Some other servants heard about this went to the king, and told him all that had happened. How did the king respond the second time?

_____

_____

_____

Jesus' words are a little strong in verse 35. He said, "That's what my heavenly Father will do to you if you refuse to forgive your brothers and sisters from your heart." If we are not careful, our acts of unforgiveness become a prison for our hearts.

> "Never forget the three powerful resources you always have available to you: love, prayer and forgiveness" (H. Jackson Brown, Jr.).

In Week One, I had you write a description about how you feel about the fruit in your life (needs improvement, nonexistent, struggling, etc.). Without looking back at what you wrote weeks ago, write down what first comes to mind below.

Love: _____

Joy: _____

Peace: _____

Patience: _____

Kindness: _____

Goodness: _____

Faithfulness: _____

Gentleness: _____

Self-control: _____

In our first week together, we also looked at the list of the enemy's fruit. Look at this list again and make some notes next to each word. Write down what comes to mind as you go through this list.

Hate: _____

Sadness: _____

Disorder: _____

Impatience: _____

Unkindness: _____

Immorality: _____

Disloyalty: _____

Abruptness: _____

Rashness: _____

Now, go back to Week One and find your lists again. What, if anything, looks different on your fruit of the Spirit list?

_____

_____

Now, look at the counterfeit that the enemy tries to trap you in. What, if anything, looks different on your current list?

_____

_____

What has stood out to you the most in this study about your state of forgiveness and/or unforgiveness?

_____

Has the Lord required you to confront some things that you thought you were completely over and/or perhaps no longer thought about?

_____

_____

Have you had any relationships restored during the course of this study?

_____

_____

Going forward, how can you keep yourself from getting into a position of holding unforgiveness in your heart?

_____

Going forward, what, if anything, will you change about how you extend forgiveness to others?

_____

_____

Proverbs 25:28 says, "A man without self-control is like a city broken into and left without walls." As believers in Jesus Christ, we have to be people who act in a Spirit-controlled, Light-bearing manner. We need to fortify the walls of our hearts and clean out whatever does not need to be there any longer. If it is forgiveness you need to extend, do it today. If it is forgiveness you need to receive, seek it in prayer. Jesus can forgive you, and He can also move the heart of someone who has sinned against you. That person may never come to you and say, "Please forgive me," but that is okay. Move forward and release that person through prayer. Keep your eyes focused on Jesus, who is the One who extends forgiveness.

"I formed you; you are my servant; O Israel, you will not be forgotten by me. I have blotted out your transgressions like a cloud and your sins like mist; return to me, for I have redeemed you" (Isaiah 44:21–22).

> *Father, thank You for Your mercies that are new each and every morning. Thank You, Father, for each person who has been brave enough to discuss and study the concepts of forgiveness and unforgiveness. Lord Jesus, work in my heart to show me where I need to extend forgiveness and receive forgiveness. Holy Spirit, lead me each and every day so that I can surrender my rashness into your control. Lord Jesus, may I be a Spirit-filled believer, filled with Your Love and Light everywhere I go and in every relationship that I have. May I never allow the bitter root of unforgiveness to be in my life for the remainder of my days on this earth. Thank You, Jesus, for Your ultimate sacrifice on the Cross so that my sins may be completely forgiven. In Jesus' name, Amen.*

My prayer for you, friend, is that this study has freed you from any unforgiveness you may have been holding onto. I pray that the bondage that once bound you has been loosed in the name of Jesus. I pray that as you walk along your path that you operate in the fruit of the Spirit in all times and that you walk in a constant state of forgiveness because the Father has completely forgiven you. Thank you for embarking on this journey with me.

Many blessings,
Erin

Leader Guide and Discussion Questions

"Forgiveness is not an occasional act; it is a permanent attitude" (Dr. Martin Luther King, Jr).

Forgiveness is personal. It is personal because Jesus extends forgiveness to each one of us *personally*. As Dr. Martin Luther King, Jr. stated, it is also a permanent attitude. For some taking this study, they are better than others at receiving and offering forgiveness. While others, may struggle with forgiveness or not quite fully understand it. Know that both are okay , and that may be the reason why an individual is taking this study in the first place.

Tips for promoting a healthy environment within your group:

1. As the leader, allow yourself to be transparent. Your group members are not going to want to share if you do not.
2. Be respectful of each member's responses. Some of your group members may be coming from a place of immense hurt or sorrow. If a discussion moment during your time together gets to be a bit

too much, perhaps you can call for a short break to speak to your group member and allow them to compose themselves.
3. Do not allow any one member to monopolize your time together.
4. Allow for silent times—your group members may be reflecting, thinking of an answer, praying, or are just plain too nervous to answer.
5. Be a good listener and do not offer free advice. In some cases, referrals for counseling may be needed. Be sure you have resources on hand to refer them to.
6. Respect your group members' time. Do your best to start on time and end on time.
7. Briefly discuss the prior week's homework before you can begin the new lesson. This will help you understand how your members are working through the lesson as well as see how Jesus is working in their lives.
8. Be okay with the fact that not all forgiveness issues may be resolved with this one study. If possible, stay in contact with those in your group, especially ones you know are struggling with forgiveness/unforgiveness.
9. Enjoy your time in His Word!

Use these questions each week to facilitate discussion within your small group.

Week One Discussion Questions

1. At what point in your life did you fully understand what took place on the Cross? Describe your life at that point. If you do not yet understand, what questions do you still have?
2. Would you say that you are a "control" person? How does that affect your ability to extend forgiveness?
3. What led you to take this study, and what do you hope to get out of this group study?

Week Two Discussion Questions

1. Do you really think you can have a love/hate relationship?
2. Is the love you extend conditional?
3. If not everyone loves Jesus and He commanded us to love (as the second greatest commandment), how should we respond when people do not love us? How did Jesus respond?

Week Three Discussion Questions

1. Have you or anyone you known battled with depression? What was at the root of the depression?
2. Discuss a time when you experienced great joy even in the midst of a difficult relationship or life issue.
3. Are there things in your life that are causing you sadness that could be turned into joyful things, given the right perspective and attitude change? Expand.

Week Four Discussion Questions

1. Be honest; do you thrive more in chaotic environments or in peaceful environments? Why?
2. If names have meaning, especially in the Bible, what is your favorite name for God? Why?
3. The donkey represents peace in the Bible (*see* John 12:15). What animal represents your current life situation?

Week Five Discussion Questions

1. When it comes to patience, are you "running on empty" or are you more like a nurturing preschool teacher?
2. How hard is it for you to wait on God's timing? How do you think this relates to your attitude toward God?
3. Is there something you are angry with God about? Have you taken it to Him, or do you think He is not approachable about the subject?

Week Six Discussion Questions

1. Describe a time when someone was unkind to you. How did you respond?
2. When someone is kind to you, how does that make you feel?
3. Why is it hard for us to be kind to those who have hurt us? Why do you think that is?

Use these questions each week to facilitate discussion within your small group.

Week Seven Discussion Questions

1. How do you respond when someone asks you, "If God is good, why does bad happen?"
2. Describe the difference between how God sees you and how Satan sees you.
3. If knowing unforgiveness can block the Holy Spirit's work in and through you, how does unforgiveness allow Satan to have a toehold into your soul?

Week Eight Discussion Questions

1. What is the difference between God's definition of *faithful* and the world's definition of *faithful*?
2. Describe a time, if any, when you felt your faith being shaken or possibly when you felt you lacked faith?
3. Discuss Charles Stanley's quote, "Sometimes the most difficult person to pardon is oneself, but forgiveness is never complete until that has happened." What does this mean to you?

Week Nine Discussion Questions

1. Discuss a time when you felt the gentleness of Jesus.
2. How does gentleness and our ability to see others through Jesus' eyes relate to how you treat others?
3. Describe a time when God confronted you about your abrupt behavior toward someone? What was the end result?

Week Ten Discussion Questions

1. Would you say you are more "self-controlled" or "Spirit-controlled?" Why?
2. Of all the fruit of the Spirit, which one is your strongest, and which one is your weakest?
3. Discuss how God has moved you from unforgiveness to forgiveness during this study.

Endnotes

1 Matthew 7:13.
2 "love." *Merriam-Webster.com.* 2014. http://www.merriam-webster.com/dictionary/love (1 June 2014)
3 "hate." *Merriam-Webster.com.* 2014. http://www.merriam-webster.com/dictionary/hate (1 June 2014)
4 Matthew 22:35–36, New Living Translation.
5 Matthew 22:37, New Living Translation.
6 Matthew 22:39, New Living Translation.
7 http://www.everydayhealth.com/health-report/major-depression/depression-statistics.aspx; retrieved 9 June 2014.
8 "sad." *Merriam-Webster.com.* 2014. http://www.merriam-webster.com/dictionary/sad (29 June 2014)
9 "joy." *Merriam-Webster.com.* 2014. http://www.merriam-webster.com/dictionary/joy (29 June 2014)
10 Job 1:21, New Living Translation.
11 Genesis 3:1–13, New Living Translation.
12 *See* Matthew 6:14.
13 "forgive." *Merriam-Webster.com.* 2014. http://www.merriam-webster.com/dictionary/forgive (9 July 2014)
14 http://en.wikipedia.org/wiki/Helen_Keller

15   *Strong's Concordance*, s.v. Hebrew 1136 *chesed*, http://biblesuite.com/hebrew/1136.htm
16   New Living Translation.
17   Colossians 3:12–13.
18   *Strong's Concordance*, s.v. Hebrew 2896 *towb*, http://biblesuite.com/hebrew/2896.htm
19   "After a Malaysian Plane is Shot Down in Ukraine, grief and outrage ripple worldwide," http://m.washingtonpost.com/world/after-a-malaysian-plane-is-shot-down-in-ukraine-grief-and-outrage-ripple-worldwide/2014/07/24/b9bf99a2-11e9-11e4-98ee-daea85133bc9_story.html, Retrieved on 25 July 2014
20   John 13:34.
21   Psalm 31:19.
22   *Strong's Concordance*, s.v., Greek 4103, *pistos*, http://www.blueletterbible.org/lang/lexicon/lexicon.cfm?Strongs=G4103&t=ESV
23   *Strong's Concordance*, s.v., Hebrew 539 *'aman*, http://www.blueletterbible.org/lang/lexicon/lexicon.cfm?Strongs=H539&t=ESV
24   *Strong's Concordance*, s.v., Greek 569, *apisteō* http://www.blueletterbible.org/lang/lexicon/lexicon.cfm?Strongs=G569&t=ESV
25   *Strong's Concordance*, s.v., Greek 5485, *charis* http://www.blueletterbible.org/lang/lexicon/lexicon.cfm?Strongs=G5485&t=ESV
26   Acts 3:19.
27   John 4:28–30, 39.
28   John 4:29.
29   *Strong's Concordance*, s.v., Greek 1466, *egkráteia*, http://www.blueletterbible.org/lang/lexicon/lexicon.cfm?Strongs=G1466&t=ESV
30   *Strong's Concordance*, s.v., Hebrew 981, *bata' or batah*, http://www.blueletterbible.org/lang/lexicon/lexicon.cfm?Strongs=H981&t=ESV
31   Ephesians 1:4–5, New Living Translation, *emphasis mine*.

CPSIA information can be obtained
at www.ICGtesting.com
Printed in the USA
LVOW10s1229051117
555097LV00013B/473/P